THE ROMAN VERGIL

AND THE ORIGINS
OF MEDIEVAL BOOK DESIGN

THE ROMAN VERGIL

AND THE ORIGINS
OF MEDIEVAL BOOK DESIGN

David H. Wright

UNIVERSITY OF TORONTO PRESS

TABLE OF CONTENTS

Frontispiece: Dido and Aeneas in the cave, to illustrate Book IV of the *Aeneid* (actual size)

When it was produced for a very wealthy patron in Rome towards the end of the fifth century, the Roman Vergil (now Vatican Library, Vat. lat. 3867) was an enormous book of 410 folios of the very finest parchment, measuring about 350 by 335 mm, containing all the commonly accepted works of Vergil: the ten short *Eclogues*, each with a small illustration at the head of the text, the four books of the *Georgics*, each preceded by a pair of illustrations on a separate bifolium of parchment, and then the twelve books of the *Aeneid*, each also preceded by a pair of illustrations. It was made for luxurious display. Losses during the Middle Ages have deprived us of about a quarter of the text, three of the *Eclogue* illustrations, six of the eight *Georgics* illustrations, and fourteen of the twenty-four *Aeneid* illustrations, but it remains the most impressive example we have of Roman book illumination at the moment of transition from classical to medieval practices.

The essential purpose of this publication is to present the Roman Vergil in such a way that the reader can appreciate its art in its historical context. Therefore the Presentation section gives all the illustrations in colour, together with the unique framed *incipit* page for the *Aeneid* and good examples of a colophon and of a verse summary page with their modest ornament. This is accompanied by a brief commentary explaining the subjects of the illustrations, including quotations from Vergil as appropriate, and a few comments on their artistic qualities. Unfortunately the manuscript is so enormous that even with our large page size it is possible to give these reproductions at only 80% of actual size, so the reader must always enlarge them in imagination to understand the patron's intentions.

As background before the Presentation section there is a brief general chapter on the history and art of Rome in the fifth century, illustrated by a sequence of five official ivory diptychs showing the transformation of classical figure style that took place during this period and led to what we see in the Roman Vergil. Then after the Presentation section there is a chapter on the materials and procedures used in making the manuscript, including a close analysis of its remarkably elaborate script, and notes on the innovations in book design here that constitute a long step in the direction of medieval book decoration. Next there is a chapter on the iconographic tradition of Vergil illustrations, comparing the smaller but fully illustrated "Vatican Vergil" produced in Rome around 400, and considering also other iconographic traditions upon which the artist of the Roman Vergil drew: the general repertory of bucolic scenes, the tradition of author portraits, and an important reflection of imperial representation. Then comes an examination of stylistic developments in fifth-century painting, comparing mosaics in Rome and Ravenna, and placing the Roman Vergil at the end of that sequence. The concluding section seeks to bring all these lines of investigation together to achieve a balanced appreciation of the Roman Vergil in the larger context of cultural history. At the end there is a brief annotated list of current bibliography on all these topics.

In modern times the Roman Vergil has long been studied for its text but very little for its illustrations. In 1893 the great Viennese scholar Franz Wickhoff, the principal founder of the Viennese school of Kunstgeschichte, suggested that it was made for schoolboys, with deliberately clear lettering and simplified illustrations that would appeal to them; more recently it has generally been dismissed as provincial work of the fifth or sixth centuries.

I first encountered the book in 1950 in a lecture course with Wilhelm Koehler, the renowned specialist on Carolingian manuscripts and himself a pupil of Wickhoff; he emphasized the extremely fine quality of book production seen here, especially the parchment, and denied a provincial origin. I have followed up Koehler's insights, confirming and deepening them, to reach the conclusions presented here. The next year I followed the lectures and seminars of Heinz Kähler in Munich; he never mentioned manuscripts but gave me much deeper insight into the continuity and innovations of Late Antique art. Since 1956 I have always relied on the friendship and example of Ernst Kitzinger, and for a couple of years beginning in 1960 I was informally associated with E. A. Lowe, whose connoisseurship of early manuscripts is legendary. In later years I have been deeply indebted to the friendship and advice of Bernhard Bischoff and Florentine Mütherich. I remember also with affection and respect many conversations with Carl Nordenfalk but I have not hesitated to contradict him on an issue of the highest importance to him: the date of the Augustan Vergil. In all my research in this field I have benefitted enormously from the resources of two libraries, the Warburg Institute in London and the American Academy in Rome.

My earlier book *Codicological Notes on the Vergilius Romanus* (Vatican City, 1992) benefited in innumerable details from the ingenious advice of Fr. Leonard E. Boyle, OP. Specifically for this book I have relied on the generous advice of William S. Anderson, Michelle Brown, and Scot McKendrick. David Way in London has been an ideal sponsoring editor and Giuliano Bianucci, Francesca Cinelli, Mauro Del Corpo and Luigi Riva in Milan have been wonderfully enterprising in bringing the project to fruition. The copies of Wilpert's plates of mosaics are reproduced by courtesy of the Pontificio Istituto di Archeologia Cristiana. The photograph on page 8 is reproduced by courtesy of the Rheinisches Bildarchiv, and that on page 52 is reproduced by courtesy of the Deutsches Archäologisches Institut, Rome. Don Raffaele Farina, SDB, Prefect of the Biblioteca Apostolica Vaticana, has kindly authorized the publication, and I want also to thank the members of the library staff for innumerable courtesies, beginning with my first visit in 1952.

Rome at the end of the fourth century enjoyed relative prosperity, political stability, and a great revival of classical culture, but during the fifth century there was a long process of decline, punctuated by the Visigothic sack of 410 and the Vandal sack of 455. Emperors had for some time been based in Milan, but in 402 Honorius moved to Ravenna for safety; only for brief periods in the middle of the century was there an Emperor or a pretender in Rome. The Senate remained an important part of the political system at the beginning of the century but it gradually dwindled in effectiveness while remaining symbolically important. The Bishop became the principal civic authority while also asserting universal authority in the Church; indeed, Innocent I (401-17) took such strong action that he is commonly considered the first to deserve the title Pope. Celestine I (422-32) and Sixtus III (432-40) were important patrons of art and Leo I (440-61) was a dominant political leader in his time. Meanwhile a succession of Germanic peoples invaded the northern and western provinces, and then north-western Africa; imperial administration collapsed in those provinces and the former organized Roman army vanished to be replaced by mercenary forces of Germans or Huns led by generals who were themselves of Germanic origin. At the same time the separation from the more stable eastern half of the Empire deepened step by step.

Membership in the Senate still carried great prestige but had little authority. Three times during the fifth century a Roman senator was a short-lived claimant to the imperial throne. Priscus Attalus, a pagan in the circle of Symmachus, the leading pagan orator, negotiated Rome's enormous ransom with the Visigoth Alaric in 408, became Prefect of Rome, and then in further negotiation when Alaric again besieged Rome the next year agreed to claim the imperial title and go with Alaric to unseat the incompetent Honorius in Ravenna; their expedition failed and Attalus withdrew, pardoned by Honorius in June 410. But since Alaric did not get the payment he demanded he returned and sacked defenceless Rome that August. There was a period of confusion after the death of Honorius in 423 until his six-year old nephew Valentinian III was put on the throne in 425 with his mother Galla Placidia in charge. Then in 454 Petronius Maximus, a very wealthy senator who had twice served as consul, persuaded the incompetent Valentinian III to murder his excellent military commander Aetius, a Roman patrician, so that Petronius himself could succeed Aetius; the next year Petronius

appears to have arranged the murder of Valentinian and bought the support needed to put himself on the throne. But less than three months later Gaiseric and his Vandals, who had taken north-western Africa virtually without opposition some twenty years earlier, now approached Rome; Petronius attempted to flee but was caught and murdered by a furious Roman crowd. After another period of usurpation and confusion, in 472 Olybrius, a member of the distinguished Anicius family who had fled to Constantinople in 455 and who was married to the daughter of Valentinian III, returned to claim the throne with the support of the Suevian Ricimer, the most powerful military commander of the time, who had already made and unmade three emperors; but Olybrius died of dropsy after six months. Such a series of miserable incidents vividly illustrates the collapse of the traditional imperial system in the west and the lack of leadership in the Senate.

Yet Rome remained not only the traditional capital but also by far the largest city in the Empire, with a population probably of well over half a million. The surviving original parts of the enormous basilica of S. Maria Maggiore reveal the art patronage of Sixtus III (432-40) on a scale worthy of one of the great emperors of the past. Apart from the affairs of the Popes recorded in the *Liber pontificalis* we know very little about the wealthiest class and their art patronage in the second half of the century. We should note that the famous struggles of the period involved the collapsed northern frontier and the old western and north African provinces, not Rome itself, and we may suppose that the great land-owning families whose lands did not lie in territories ravaged by invaders might remain very wealthy indeed, and able to commission a luxury manuscript like the Roman Vergil. For landmarks in art we do have a series of ivory diptychs commissioned by such patrons extending to the year 487, intended as gifts to celebrate the entry into office of members of the greatest families of the senatorial class in Rome. They are our best evidence for the course of developments in art in Rome in this era and are illustrated here at 80% of actual size, the same scale as used for the illustrations in the Roman Vergil.

To begin around 400, consider the beautifully carved diptych that celebrated the installation of Probianus as *Vicarius urbis Romae*, an imperial office of considerable importance. On both panels he is enthroned and flanked by secretaries holding open wax tablets, while below him (that is, in front of him) orators

Ivory diptych of Probianus, c. 400 (Berlin, Staatsbibliothek)

address him with their raised right hands, holding open rolls in their left hands, with fingers marking their place. On the panel at the left (actually the back of the diptych but the first in order according to the inscription) both Probianus and the orators wear the elaborate senatorial toga while on the other panel they wear the chlamys, a mantle fastened at the right shoulder, which is the costume of their office. The figures are carved in relatively high relief and are fully realized in three dimensions. They turn freely in space, the secretary at the far right seen in profile, the orator at the far left seen primarily from behind. Of course there is hierarchic scaling: Probianus is much larger than any of the others, and the secretaries are slightly smaller than the orators, but that is a normal convention in Late Antiquity. By comparison with reliefs such as those carved for Constantine a century earlier this is a very successful revival of classical style, recalling the tradition of Augustan art. The bodies are correctly proportioned and articulated. You can always tell which leg is straight and bears most of the weight, and which is bent, free to take a step. The garments fall naturally and voluminously and they reveal enough of the underlying anatomy to mark the articulation. The space of the chamber is defined by the duly foreshortened sections of receding entablature and it is not difficult for us to accept the Late Antique device of putting the foreground figures in a separate frame.

Turning next to the panel of Felix, Consul in the year 428, we find a radical change. It was carved in somewhat lower relief but with great skill, with details of the face fully modelled, but taken as a whole the figure appears flat, without substance. Not only is there no distinction between straight and bent leg but the feet appear dangling, as if hanging in the air, and the eyes are directed upwards, as if to heaven. The basic principle of classical art, ponderation (the treatment of the human body as a rationally coordinated structure organized in terms of weight and support), is now forgotten. The right elbow is articulated but the shoulders disappear beneath simplified contours; a dwarfed left shoulder is apparent because the artist wants to show the pattern of the embroidered *trabea* that passes over it, but the right shoulder is forgotten. Yet this artist who fails to articulate the body not only depicts the embroidered pattern, he even distinguishes individual folds in the stiff garment where it falls below the waist. This is excellent craftsmanship but any fundamental understanding of classical style, any capacity to invent convincing figures active in a coherent space, is gone.

Consular diptych of Felix, 428 (Paris, Bibliothèque Nationale)

In the middle of the century a remarkable ivory panel was carved showing the Apotheosis of an Emperor, probably Antoninus Pius who had died in 161, and here is commemorated in a specifically pagan manner. In the upper part the *divus* is carried aloft by two winds to join his ancestors. The nudes are well carved but the emperor has a drastically shortened torso and right arm, and there is something very strange about the flatness of his head. The face is nearly frontal but we see much of the left side of the head carved as if it were an extension of that front plane. It is a sort of squashed three-quarter view, as if two planes that should be at right angles were unfolded into a flat pattern. The difference between this effect and the coherent three-quarter views of the secretaries of Probianus is striking, for in the classical style seen there the head is understood as a solid object, while here it appears almost flattened. Two of the heads of ancestors are carved in nearly frontal views but the other heads in this part of the ivory panel are all arbitrarily simplified profiles.

The lower part of the panel is significantly different in style. The head of the seated statue of the Emperor is convincingly shown in three-quarter view; the four attendants riding the elephants are a little stubby in proportions but they turn freely in space and the heads of the two in the middle have different three-quarter views. These must all have been copied from an ancient model, probably one from the Antonine period, for that is the approximate date for the type of toga worn by the statue of the Emperor. This distinction offers an important lesson for using stylistic evidence to date works of art in this period; this sculptor was capable of repeating rather accurately most of the style of his model in the lower part of the ivory but his own style is more evident in the upper part.

Half of an ivory diptych with the Apotheosis of an Emperor, mid-fifth century (British Museum)

In 480 Basilius was Consul and the surviving upper part of one of his ivory panels is particularly significant; it shows a victory figure seated on a globe above an eagle (which is mostly missing) and holding a shield with the bust of the Consul. Her torso is drastically abbreviated and the outline of the globe is actually too high on the surface for her to be sitting on it; there is no suggestion of coherent relationships in space. Her feet dangle suspended in the air and her head is carved in a strangely distorted three-quarter view. Classical iconography lies behind this carving and the technique is respectable, but there is nothing left of classical figure style. The pattern of the drapery between her legs is strikingly like that of several frontal enthroned figures in the Roman Vergil (see pp. 16, 18, 20 and 32).

The diptych of Boethius (next page), Consul in 487 (and father of the great philosopher), carries this stylistic evolution a step further. Compared with Felix in 428 this standing figure has no shoulders at all and the folds of the cloak drawn across his waist now fall in the same schematic pattern as in the victory figure on the ivory of Basilius. The arms and shoulders of the seated figure are like the *divus* carried aloft, but stiffer and with less remnant of natural anatomy, and the drapery passing across his body is made into a more arbitrary flat pattern. There is no sense of volume in this frontal seated figure, entirely unlike the representations of Probianus. The carving of decorative patterns is quite precise but the carving of the face is terribly distorted.

By this time, although a Consul was still appointed each year in the West, and the honour was still highly esteemed (for the year was still dated by the names of the Consuls), there was no longer a claimant to the imperial throne in the West. Romulus Augustus had been deposed in 476 and although his predecessor Julius Nepos still had the title Augustus, he lived in exile in Dalmatia until his death in 480. The ruler of the West was the Germanic military leader Odoacar in Ravenna, with the title Rex, until he was captured and murdered by another Germanic leader, Theoderic, in 493.

Through all this, Rome remained the largest city in the empire as well as the revered symbol of cultural traditions. The Popes kept the machinery of daily life working, at least more or less, taking responsibility, for example, for the distribution of grain. We have no detailed accounts but we can assume that some wealthy aristocrats perpetuated their society in relative isolation during this gradual decline.

Consular diptych of Basilius, 480 (Milan)

NARMANIBOETHIVSVCETINL

EXPPPVSECCONSORDETPATRIC

Consular diptych of Boethius, 487 (Brescia)

This section is designed to give the reader as nearly as possible the experience of turning the pages of the Roman Vergil. The illustrations come in their true order (though several were bound in the wrong place in the Renaissance), at the right if on a recto page, at the left if on a verso page (except that the details on pp. 18, 20 and 21 and the colophon and preface on pp. 36–7 must be placed on the wrong faces to preserve their true order). For the small illustrations of the *Eclogues* they are placed at the top or bottom of the page as they are in the manuscript. Of course the reader must imagine turning many pages of text between these illustrations, especially in the *Georgics* and the *Aeneid*, where there was originally a facing pair of illustrations at the start of each book but nothing in the rest of the text. The reader must also imagine the effect of grand demarcation between books that came from having the recto of the first illustration and the verso of the second in the pair of frontispieces left empty, sometimes a whole opening left empty before the new book started (when the text of the previous book ended on a verso and the Summary of the next book was therefore on the recto of the leaf with the blank verso that produced this grand effect). Above all the reader must remember that despite this large page size the pages of the Roman Vergil can be reproduced here at only 80% of actual size. To facilitate comparison, the same scale of reproduction is used for the ivory carvings in the first section, and for the page of the Augustan Vergil in the Conclusion. To see an illustration from the Roman Vergil at full size, look at the frontispiece, where the usual ample margins are of necessity trimmed off. The comparative illustrations of the Vatican Vergil, on the other hand, because it is a much smaller manuscript, are reproduced at actual size.

The first surviving page of the Roman Vergil has the opening lines of the first *Eclogue* and an illustration of that passage, all considerably rubbed from wear. Facing it we should assume was another folio of the same fine parchment, blank on the recto to guard against damage from the binding, and with a brief title on the verso, identifying the contents of the volume (as survives in two Carolingian copies of the lost Late Antique illustrated Terence). The *Eclogues* are a set of ten bucolic poems composed in the turbulent years around 40 B.C. when Octavian was confiscating land to settle his veterans, after his victory over Brutus and Cassius, revenging the murder of Caesar. The first of the *Eclogues*, deliberately placed in that location, is a dialogue between two herdsmen, one of whom has lost his land through confiscation, while the other sings the praises of Octavian, whose intervention saved him from confiscation. Whatever Vergil's own experience may have been in this matter, for his family had land near Mantua, where confiscations took place, the prominence of this poem must express his hopes for Octavian's protection when the *Eclogues* were published around 39-8 B.C.

Although clumsily drawn, this painting illustrates the opening lines exactly; Meliboeus, at the right, who has been expelled from his land, speaks:

TITYRE, TU PATULAE RECUBANS SUB TEGMINE FAGI	Tityrus, you relaxing beneath a spreading beech
SILVESTREM TENUI MUSAM MEDITARIS AVENA:	dwell upon the woodland muse with a thin shepherd's pipe,
NOS PATRIAE FINIS ET DULCIA LINQUIMUS ARVA;	while I abandon my native land and beloved fields;
NOS PATRIAM FUGIMUS: TU, TITYRE, LENTUS IN UMBRA	I flee my country; you, Tityrus, relaxing in the shade
FORMOSAM RESONARE DOCES AMARYLLIDA SILVAS.	teach the woods to echo the name of fair Amaryllis.

Meliboeus steps forward onto his right leg and reaches out with his right hand, two fingers extended, in a common gesture of speech. With his left hand he leads one of his goats by the horns, the goat he mentions in verses 12-15 as having just given birth to twins, the hope of the flock, but abandoned on the bare rock. Tityrus sits under a tree playing a pipe, as described, and behind him his cattle graze peacefully, as mentioned in verse 9. Both men wear the labourer's tunic, the *exomis*, belted, and tied above the left shoulder, leaving the right arm unencumbered; Meliboeus has a satchel suspended by a strap across his chest. The only departure from the text is the shape of the leaves above Tityrus, which are trilobate and cannot be a beech tree (though the leaves of the tree at the right could be).

This illustration is unique in this book in having no frame and no painted background. That fact and the accuracy of iconographic detail suggest that this illustration is copied from a much older model, perhaps directly from a painting in a papyrus roll, where heavy applications of paint for a background and frame would be impractical because they would flake off with constant handling. Such illustrations in the "papyrus style" certainly existed and it must be expected that one would have been made to decorate the first text in a roll containing works by the most renowned Roman poet; there are reflections of similar iconography in early medieval manuscripts, but none close enough to imply direct copying from this book or its model.

The execution of this painting is also by far the clumsiest in the book. Most of the outlines are drawn as thin lines but the edges of the tunics and one side of the left leg of Meliboeus are so heavy that some have thought they are later restorations; close examination at high magnification shows that this is not so, that the painter made all of these brush strokes in the same campaign. All the paintings in the manuscript are clearly by the same hand, using the same pigments and medium, but a glance through the following pages shows that the painter soon learned to improve his technique. It seems that he had been accustomed to painting on walls or large panels and had to adjust his technique to execute miniatures in a book.

Meliboeus Salutes Tityrus (first *Eclogue*, fol. 1r)

ETIAM SVMMA PROCVL VILLARVM CVLMINA FVMANT
MAIORESQVE CADVNT ALTIS DE MONTIBVS VMBRAE

POEIA CORYDON

FORMONSVM CORYDON PASTOR ARDEBAT ALEXIN
DELICIAS DOMINI NEC QVID SPERARET HABEBAT
TANTVM INTER DENSAS VMBROSA CACVMINA FAGOS
ADSIDVAE VENIEBAT IBI HAEC INCONDITA SOLVS

Author (second *Eclogue*, fol. 3v)

MENALCAS Λ DAMOETAS Λ PALAEMON

MEN DIC MIHI DAMOETA CVIVM PECVS AN MELIBOEI

DAM NON VERVM AEGONIS NVPER MIHI TRADIDIT AEGON

Palaemon with Menalcas and Damoetes (third *Eclogue*, fol. 6r)

(at the left) The second *Eclogue* is a monologue, a lament for unrequited love spoken by the herdsman Corydon, whom the title written in red below the painting identifies. But instead of a herdsman the illustration presents a generic image of an author holding a roll and flanked by a lectern and a *capsa*, a cylindrical box for rolls. His face lacks any distinctive features and stares straight ahead. He wears a long white tunic with a loose sleeve over his right arm and vertical stripes down his chest, *clavi* that could indicate rank if they were more precisely rendered, and he has a cloak wrapped behind his back and across his lap in an irrational manner. There is no reason to suppose (as some have loosely suggested) that this is in any way an actual portrait of Vergil, it is simply a clumsy rendering of a formulaic author image (see p. 52) that was then repeated for the other monologues. It is noteworthy, on the other hand, that it has a loosely painted background and a carefully drawn frame, a convention appropriate to a codex and not to a roll, but that the height of the frame is uncomfortably low while the width is dictated by the ruled vertical limits of the written space. Clearly our artist is improvising.

(above) The next poem is basically a dialogue between two herdsmen, Menalcas and Damoetas, who taunt each other and then agree to a poetic contest to be judged by a third, Palaemon, as they speak their couplets in alternation. To illustrate this our painter has improvised a bucolic setting with a grazing herd, two dogs, a herdsman's rustic shelter, and three seated herdsmen, each holding a slightly curved staff (the *pedum*) and each speaking with his right hand, two fingers extended. The two figures at the right are virtually identical but there is one significant difference in the figure at the left: his tunic has a loose sleeve; it is not the *exomis* of the active labourer who needs to have his right arm completely free. That detail marks the figure at the left as Palaemon, the judge of the contest, who speaks briefly at the beginning of the contest and at the end (declaring it to be a draw). But to have all three speaking at once is nonsense. Clearly our painter improvised by taking the figure of Tityrus from his first illustration, changing his garment, and changing his gesture from playing a flute to speaking. For the rest he has used stock figures from the repertory of bucolic decorative paintings (compare his subsequent examples and the further discussion on p. 52). His frame is again uncomfortably low, for the scribe had left very little space for this illustration even though it comes at the top of a page.

(*below*) The fourth *Eclogue* is a famous hymn in honour of the birth of a boy, with a prediction of a coming golden age, but the illustration for it is squeezed in at the bottom of the page below the last verses of the third *Eclogue*; the title *Saeculi novi interpraetatio* comes on the top line of the next page (see p. 46), where the text begins. Since this is again a mono- logue we have essentially the same generic author repeated, with the *capsa* and lectern switched around. This time the draw- ing is slightly better, for the cloak is draped across the lap in a plausible manner and the face is not severely frontal. Unfortunately, however, the artist appears to have made some error with his brown underpaint, from which the upper layer of pink and tan has worn off irregularly, giving a blotchy appearance.

Author (fourth *Eclogue*, fol. 9r)

The fifth *Eclogue* is a relatively simple dialogue, first a conversation between the herdsmen Menalcas and Mopsus, then a friendly poetic contest in which each laments the death of the herdsman Daphnis, leading to mutual compliments and an exchange of gifts. This illustration again comes at the end of the previous poem, and the title identifying the speakers is again at the top of the next page, but this time there is enough room for the illustration, and our painter's work has improved significantly. The herdsman at the left, leaning on his staff, is speaking, while the one at the right, leaning more awkwardly, is listening. That seems to show the contest in progress, when each man speaks at considerable length, but by that time they have entered a cave for shelter during their contest. This illustration, therefore, does not correspond to any specific moment in the narrative and so must again be an improvisation out of stock elements of the decorator's bucolic vocabulary, rendered with less than complete understanding.

FORMONSVALPARIBVSMODISADQVEAEREMENALCA

FMVNORVM·SATYRORVM·ETSILENORVMDELECTATIO
POE PRIMASYRACOSIODIGNATAESTLVDEREVERSV
NOSTRANEGERVBVITSILVISHABITARETHALEA
CVMCANEREMREGESETPROELIACYNTHIVSAVRE

Author (sixth *Eclogue*, fol. 14r)

(*above*) The sixth *Eclogue* is again given a generic author portrait because it is written in the voice of the poet addressing his patron Varus, but it has many narrative incidents that could well have been illustrated, beginning with the moment when the herdsmen Chromis and Mnasyllos find Silenus lying asleep in a cave and force him to entertain them with tales from mythology, many of which also suggest potential illustrations. This is implied in the long title below the illustration, characterizing the subject matter as the delectation of fauns, satyrs, and silens. Again it is evident that our painter is improvising his illustrations, in effect taking the easy path by avoiding the mythological content. His technique, on the other hand, is by now considerably improved; the composition is essentially the same as in the crowded painting for the fourth *Eclogue* but the contours of the drapery and the blending of colours in the face are more convincing.

(*at the right*) The illustration for the seventh *Eclogue* comes at the bottom of a verso and the text itself, with its title, is entirely lost. It is again a competitive dialogue between two herdsmen, Corydon and Thyrsis, narrated and judged by Meliboeus, who also mentions another herdsman, Daphnis (omitted from the illustration), as hearing the contest. Our artist has improvised this scene out of the same bucolic vocabulary he used for the fifth *Eclogue* and if he makes the two competing herdsmen speak simultaneously (as in the third *Eclogue*) the composition here makes that less disturbing. Once again the drawing of these figures is slightly more competent than in his previous version of this vocabulary. The reclining herdsman is a different motif, taken from the normal vocabulary of bucolic decoration, but his gesture and glance have been adjusted specifically for this composition.

Facing page: Corydon and Thyrsus compete before Meliboeus (seventh *Eclogue*, fol. 16v) (*referring to the next two illustrations*) There follows a loss of eight folios with the other three *Eclogue* illustrations; then the illustrations for the first two books of the *Georgics* are also lost, those for the fourth book also, probably because they were on separate bifolia, for most of these texts survive. The only illustrations we have for the *Georgics* (next opening) are the pair that characterize Book III, which concerns animal husbandry. These are not illustrations in the specific sense, for nothing shown here depicts episodes or advice given in the text, as do the illustrations for the *Georgics* in the Vatican Vergil (compare the story of the old Corycian, p. 54). The two bulls facing off at the bottom of the page at the right are a normal decorative motif, used here as an allusion to the content of this book, not specifically an illustration of the passage 3.209-41, where Vergil warns of the dangers of sexual passion among bulls and the need to keep them in isolation; in the Vatican Vergil, closely following the text, this is illustrated by showing also the beautiful cow who is the object of the combat and by showing the bull who lost going off alone to exercise himself in preparation for renewed combat.

The bucolic motifs used here are the same as in the previous odd-numbered *Eclogues*, with the addition of gambolling horses, a mare and her foal, and the confronted bulls, but not of the cows that are also prominent in Vergil's advice. The relaxed standing herdsman leaning on his staff is relatively well drawn, probably copied directly from a decorator's model book; the herdsman seated at the right reaches out with his right hand open, palm up, in a gesture that means accepting what is said (compare the Vatican Vergil, p. 54), perhaps meaning here general acceptance of Vergil's advice. The composition here is absolutely flat, for every object is seen in profile, there is great disparity of scale, and there is no significant overlap to establish relationships in space. The landscape no longer has a horizon, as it did in the *Eclogue* landscapes. All the motifs are scattered around in a system long customary in the design of mosaic pavements, but our painter's brushwork is too irregular to give the even background expected in mosaics, while on the other hand he makes no effort to depict the irregularities of actual ground. In the fifth *Eclogue* illustration, and more successfully in the seventh, he does depict the grass of a field and he distinguishes that from the sky above. Here he has adopted purely the decorator's approach for this improvised illustration (compare p. 53).

Herdsmen and Flocks, left half (*Georgics* III, fol. 44v)

Herdsmen and Flocks, right half (*Georgics* III, fol. 45r)

For the opening of the *Aeneid* only the right half of the original pair of illustrations survives. This shows the storm at sea, *Aen.* 1.81-123. More specifically, this illustration shows the response of Aeneas to the rising storm in verses 93-6:

INGEMIT ET DUPLICIS TENDENS AD SIDERA PALMAS	he groaned, and raising both hands to the stars
TALIA VOCE REFERT: "O TERQUE QUATERQUE BEATI,	he cried out, "Oh thrice and four times blessed
QUIS ANTE ORA PATRUM TROIAE SUB MOENIBUS ALTIS	those who before the eyes of their fathers beneath the high walls of Troy
CONTINGIT OPPETERE!" ...	were fated to meet their death!"

That is exactly the action of Aeneas here, as the rain pours down, the wind gods in the upper corners blow, and the winged female personification of the storm holds torches to suggest lightning. The mast of the nearer ship has broken and seems to be collapsing, while that of the further ship is lowered, also collapsing. If the active figures are reasonably convincing, more elaborately so than in any of our painter's previous work, we must accept as conventional abbreviation the stiff rows of standing Trojans in the two ships, and allowing for clumsy rendering we can imagine an iconographically correct miniature serving a model; three miniatures in the Vatican Vergil show ships in an appropriate manner, with tiny figures in them and a clearly receding sea (p. 49), though none happens to show a storm.

Of course we recognize the traits of our painter in the stiff attitudes of the standing Trojans and the formulaic faces, either in profile or nearly frontal, but we must also recognize a very unusual error in his work: the cloak of Aeneas is wrongly shown as clumped up on his right shoulder, as a result of raising his arms, and fastened at his left shoulder. It is an invariable rule in Roman art that cloaks are fastened at the right shoulder so as to leave the right arm free; both the other Trojans and the winds are correct in this detail, even if the drawing is rather clumsy in some of them. This error is more than simple clumsiness but there is a precedent for it in the irrationally draped cloak of our painter's first author figure.

Another feature here seems out of place, the two sea monsters and the three fish that are hopelessly out of scale; they are in fact part of a normal decorative vocabulary and must have been added by our painter to fill out the bottom part of this square composition. Thus we should imagine the iconographic model as a framed painting with a painted background, in horizontal format, very similar to the miniatures in the Vatican Vergil. For his first *Eclogue* our painter worked from a miniature in papyrus style, probably representing a very old iconography; here he was studying a codex, probably only two or three generations old.

The surviving folio of parchment here was not ruled for text and must have been half of an inserted bifolium, an arrangement that survives for the third book of the *Georgics* and the second and tenth books of the *Aeneid*. At the left of what was designed as a splendid display opening there must have been another illustration, an earlier episode. In the first part of this book there is only one readily illustratable episode, where Juno, determined to prevent Aeneas from reaching Italy, goes to King Aeolus, who has charge of the winds, and asks him to send a storm to destroy the ships of Aeneas, bribing Aeolus by promising him her most beautiful nymph in marriage. If that was the subject of the lost illustration we realize our painter must have extracted the first two illustrations of Book I from their proper place in the text, where illustrations always come in the Vatican Vergil, to combine them as a grand opening for display, an arrangement that survives here in Book II.

The Storm at Sea (*Aen.* 1.84–101, fol. 77r)

The text of the *Georgics* ended on a verso page, with a colophon like the one reproduced on page 36; next came a recto page with prefatory verses summarizing the first book of the *Aeneid*, like the verses illustrated on page 37. The verso of that leaf and the facing recto of the lost first illustration to the first Book were both left blank, to make an impressive demarcation between these books, and the verso of the second illustration is also blank. But the text of the *Aeneid* begins with special decoration on the recto facing that blank: the first three lines of text are in red and there is a decorative frame around the whole text. Using red for the first three lines was a normal way to begin a fine book written in capital script in Late Antiquity, but the frame is an entirely new idea. The design is a simple set of curving elements such as those used for the top of the Apotheosis ivory (p. 10) and commonly used in wall decoration, but here it is clumsily used: the design is repeated exactly at left and right when one would expect it to be flipped over to make a symmetrical design for the frame as a whole.

(referring to the next pair of illustrations) Book II begins with its grand opening intact, two facing illustrations on a separate bifolium of parchment that was not ruled for text. At the left is Dido's banquet, the scene at the start of the book, and at the right is the first illustratable episode in the story of the fall of Troy, the discovery of the Trojan horse, as Aeneas then explains it to the Queen. The last part of Book I describes the vast throng of Trojans and Tyrians (Dido's people in Carthage) at the sumptuous feast, and quotes Dido's toast, but here we have only the chief protagonists, Aeneas, Dido, and youthful Ascanius, the son of Aeneas, reclining around a C-shaped couch (though the youth actually is Cupid in disguise, sent by Venus to soften Dido's heart). Aeneas raises his hand to speak (begining in verse 3), leaning on his left arm, where both drapery and anatomy are badly distorted. Dido also raises her hand in speech, presumably referring to her request for the narrative, and looks to the right at the youthful Ascanias/Cupid. Her anatomy and drapery are reasonable, if compressed, but the youth's body is hopelessly confused. Below, two servants shown at a much smaller scale approach with goblet and pitchers; they are shown in profile at the bottom of the composition, presumably in the foreground, but the one at the left seems to be handing a goblet to the figures at the table. We find here two aspects of style common in the late fifth century: differences in size of figures according to rank, and a spatial construction in layers that have no clear relation to each other.

The second miniature illustrates a long passage beginning at verse 57 where the Greek Sinon is found with his hands bound behind him and brought before King Priam; he explains that he had been prepared to be sacrificed in order that the Greeks could safely leave (as required by an oracle), but that he had escaped and hidden, and now he gives an elaborate story persuading the Trojans to accept the horse as a gift to Minerva. Priam is shown speaking to Sinon, and above, watching from the wall, are five more Trojan soldiers and two women, presumably Hecuba and Cassandra, who are not actually mentioned in this passage, but whose presence is easily inferred. Again there is hierarchic scaling, but the anatomy is comprehensible if clumsy in the nude Sinon and the expressively elongated right arm of Priam.

The pairing of these two miniatures as the frontispiece to Book II may strike us as odd, but it is perfectly logical. They were the first two illustrations to this Book in the older manuscript that our artist was studying as a model. The banquet scene belongs above verse 1 and Priam and Sinon belong above verse 57, and as was true for the Storm at Sea both presumably had a horizontal format. Our artist changed both into large squares to make an effective frontispiece and then he skipped all the other illustrations there must have been in the rest of Book II. If we simply review the text we might suppose that the phase of this episode just before the appearance of Sinon, where Laocoön hurls his spear at the horse, might have been chosen instead, but that is a very brief incident and the story of Laocoön is more important for the episode after Sinon's story, where Laocoön is killed by serpents. So it seems safe to suppose our artist simply extracted the first and second illustrations in his model.

Framed text: *Aeneid* 1.1–18 (fol. 78r)

27

Dido's Banquet, left frontispiece to *Aeneid* II (*Aen.* 2.1–2, fol. 100v)

Sinon Comes Before Priam, right frontispiece to *Aeneid* II (*Aen.* 2.57-75, fol. 101r)

For Book IV only the second of the original pair of frontispiece miniatures survives, but it is perhaps the most expressive illustration in the Roman Vergil: the story of Dido and Aeneas in the cave, told in verses 160-8.

INTEREA MAGNA MISCERI MURMURE CAELUM
INCIPIT; INSEQUITUR COMMIXTA GRANDINE NIMBUS,
ET TYRII COMITES PASSIM ET TROIANA IUVENTUS
DARDANIUSQUE NEPOS VENERIS DIVERSA PER AGROS
TECTA METU PETIERE; RUUNT DE MONTIBUS AMNES.
SPELUNCAM DIDO DUX ET TROIANUS EANDEM
DEVENIUNT. PRIMA ET TELLUS ET PRONUBA JUNO
DANT SIGNUM; FULSERE IGNES ET CONSCIUS AETHER
CONUBIIS, SUMMOQUE ULULARUNT VERTICE NYMPHAE.

Meanwhile a great rumbling of storm in the sky
began; there followed rain mixed with hail;
both Tyrian retinue and Trojan youth
and the Dardan grandson of Venus variously in fields
sought shelter; torrents came down from the hills.
To the same cave Dido and the Trojan leader
found their way. Both primal Earth and nuptial Juno
gave the sign; flashing lightning and sky consented
to the union, and on the mountain top nymphs howled.

Dido and Aeneas are seated in the cave, presented frontally; there are awkward details of anatomy and drapery but there can be no mistaking the meaning. Dido's left arm is hidden behind the right arm of Aeneas, but her left hand is seen on his left shoulder, and she reaches out to him with her open right hand. Dido's shoulders are shifted to the right with respect to her knees, which are shifted slightly to the right with respect to her feet; she is clearly taking the lead in this seduction, for Cupid has worked the will of Venus on her. Aeneas has placed his right arm around Dido's shoulder, but with his torso shifted a little to the right and with his left hand clutching his cloak by his hip he is hesitating, perhaps mindful of his duty to sail on to Italy.

The cave seems like an amorphous box closing in upon the lovers, detached from the rest of the landscape; the shield and spear of Aeneas lean against it at the right but Dido's shield at the left interrupts the edge of the cave as if floating in the air. Above the cave is a seated Trojan shown against a dark area that must be some other cave or shelter but is not rationally connected to the rest of the landscape. In the left half of the composition are various elements appropriate to the subject, each one comprehensible, but not coordinated in space. The tree to which the horses are tethered reaches down almost to the frame but the horses are shown higher up, well back on what we assume is a receding ground plane, beyond some scattered branches. Those are a reminder of the decorative system of scattering elements on a neutral ground, common in late Roman mosaic pavements, and the basic system of composition in the pair of *Georgics* illustrations (pp. 22-3). We must suppose that our artist started with a more coherent composition in his model, probably in horizontal format, with better anatomy and drapery in the figures and with rational relationships in space. He copied the figures acceptably, with better understanding than in some of his previous attempts, but in rearranging them to fit this square composition he returned to his training as a decorator of walls or floors and scattered these elements around to fill the flat square on the page. This is when Late Antique painting begins to look medieval.

Dido and Aeneas Take Refuge in the Cave (*Aen.* 4.160–168, fol. 106r)

Sacrifice in Honour of Anchises (*Aen.* 5.42–103, fol. 76v misbound)

For Book V we have the left half of the original pair of frontispieces, showing the sacrifice in honour of Anchises, the first noteworthy episode in the Book and one central to the theme of the funeral games narrated there. In the foreground at the left a man dressed like the servants in Dido's banquet raises a knife to stab again the neck of a sheep, which is already bleeding. In the background is a tomb and from its open door comes a large snake, its head reaching in front of the servant, apparently about to attack the sheep. This corresponds loosely to part of the description in verses 84-93, where a giant snake comes from the tomb to sample the offerings Aeneas has laid out in *paterae* and goblets. But no such implements are shown here, and in verses 96-7, after the serpent has returned to the tomb, it is Aeneas himself who sacrifices two sheep, two pigs, and two bullocks.

But the main part of this illustration is far more puzzling. The three seated men are identified as Trojans by their Phrygian caps, and as rulers by dress, throne, and nimbus; the one in the centre appears to be presiding, since his hand is raised a little further in a gesture of speech and since the one at the left looks toward him (while the one at the right looks slightly to the left). The central figure looks at the scene of sacrifice, apparently authorizing it, and therefore should be interpreted as Aeneas; his youthful son Ascanius, at this stage in the story characterized as a full participant, should be one of the others. The only reasonable choice for the third seems to be Acestes, the local ruler in Sicily and generous host of Aeneas. He was the son of a river god and a Trojan mother and is described earlier (verse 37) as wearing a Lybian bearskin but perhaps he could be assimilated to the Trojans and given a Phrygian cap. At any rate there is nothing in the narrative to suggest this configuration, not even a moment in this episode when Aeneas could have sat down.

In front of this mysterious trio of rulers are two pairs of golden branches and two pairs of golden diadems, presumably prizes for the coming games. But in the narrative the prizes are laid out only later, after a week of feasting, and they are described as sacred tripods, arms, purple garments, gold and silver, as well as palms and crowns (verses 110-12). In the visual language of Late Antiquity enthroned figures like these, with generic prizes below them, normally depict joint emperors (as in the gold medallion of Valentinian I and Valens, p. 53) and figures without the nimbus or the high back to the throne might be Consuls or other sponsors presiding at games. Anyone looking at this illustration late in the fifth century surely would have recognized the attributes of imperial authority.

So it seems we have an image of the highest secular authority authorizing a pagan sacrifice, to interpret it in fifth-century terms. Since this image does not correspond closely to the narrative, and is not a direct illustration of text (as are all the other *Aeneid* miniatures), that pro-pagan interpretation must have suggested itself to a beholder late in the fifth century, when all pagan observances were strictly forbidden. In the Vatican Vergil, made at a time when imperial authority was only beginning to enforce the Church's strictures, there is a scene of Aeneas performing a sacrifice before entering the underworld (*Aen.* 6.249-50, p. 49) that illustrates the text exactly and therefore could provoke no objections from Christian critics and could have no personal significance for pagan defenders. Here it seems our artist, presumably at the request of the patron, has taken only the small part at the left from the older manuscript he was copying for the other *Aeneid* illustrations and has inserted for the main part an imperial composition adapted only to the extent of the Phrygian caps that identify the authorities as Trojan. This must have been a deliberate statement in favour of pagan traditions.

For Book VII we have only the right half of the original pair of frontispieces. It depicts a crucial moment in the story, near the middle of the Book, after King Latinus has welcomed the Trojans, when Ascanius, out hunting, shoots a stag that turns out to be the tame pet of Silvia, daughter of the royal gamekeeper; this provokes an outbreak of fighting between the Trojans and the Latins that leads to the full-scale war narrated in the rest of the *Aeneid*. Ascanius is stepping forward and drawing an arrow on his bow while the stag is running away to the right, an arrow already in his flank. In the upper left corner, in an area severely damaged by spilled liquid, are two medallions; the one at the right shows Diana, identified by the crescent moon above her head, while the other is probably Hercules, identified by the club. Diana is obviously appropriate to accompany the hunt, Hercules less evidently so, but there is a further meaning in the text here, for Vergil says (verses 497-8):

ASCANIUS CURVO DEREXIT SPICULA CORNU;	Ascanius with his curved bow aimed an arrow
NEC DEXTRAE ERRANTI DEUS AFUIT	nor did the deity fail to guide his uncertain aim.

In short, Allecto acting at the behest of Juno, as explained earlier in the episode, promoted this fateful turn of events.

There is a good deal of anatomical confusion here; Ascanius is stepping forward onto his right foot and his hips are therefore seen partly from behind, but his shoulders are seen in nearly frontal view, requiring an impossible twist in the middle of his torso, and the man at the right raising his shield for no apparent reason is seen from behind, but his legs are poorly attached, his neck is strangely turned, and it does not make sense for his cloak to be drawn aside in this action. Still, the essential action is clear and the other Trojans at the left are convincing; they must have been copied from the corresponding illustration in the same model in more classical style that we have seen used before. But the spatial composition again has been transformed by the decorator's strewn ground device: flowers, trees, and a quiver are scattered about, never overlapping, never establishing a continuous receding ground, without any horizon, comparable in these features to the composition of the illustration to Book III of the *Georgics*. We assume the stag is some distance away, and he is somewhat reduced in scale, but in the model we should suppose there was a coherent landscape setting, presumably in horizontal format.

(referring to pp. 36-37) At the end of the *Eclogues* and after each book of the *Georgics* and the *Aeneid* there was a colophon like the one reproduced here, with words and simple pen-drawn ornament alternately in red and in ink. It was the discovery of these colophons in 1484 that enabled the Florentine scholar Poliziano to argue the correct spelling of Vergil's name.

Following each colophon was a page given to prefatory verses summarizing the next book, with more pen-drawn ornament, as reproduced here. Then followed on a separate inserted bifolium the pair of frontispiece illustrations, and then on the next recto the beginning of the book — an arrangement amounting to a series of display pages appropriate to the luxurious nature of this codex. The specific elements of these decorated colophons were normal in fine books at this time, but the arrangement here is more sumptuous, and this is the only ancient manuscript of Vergil to include the verse prefaces (which became common in the Carolingian era).

Ascanius Shoots the Stag (*Aen.* 7.496–499, fol. 163r)

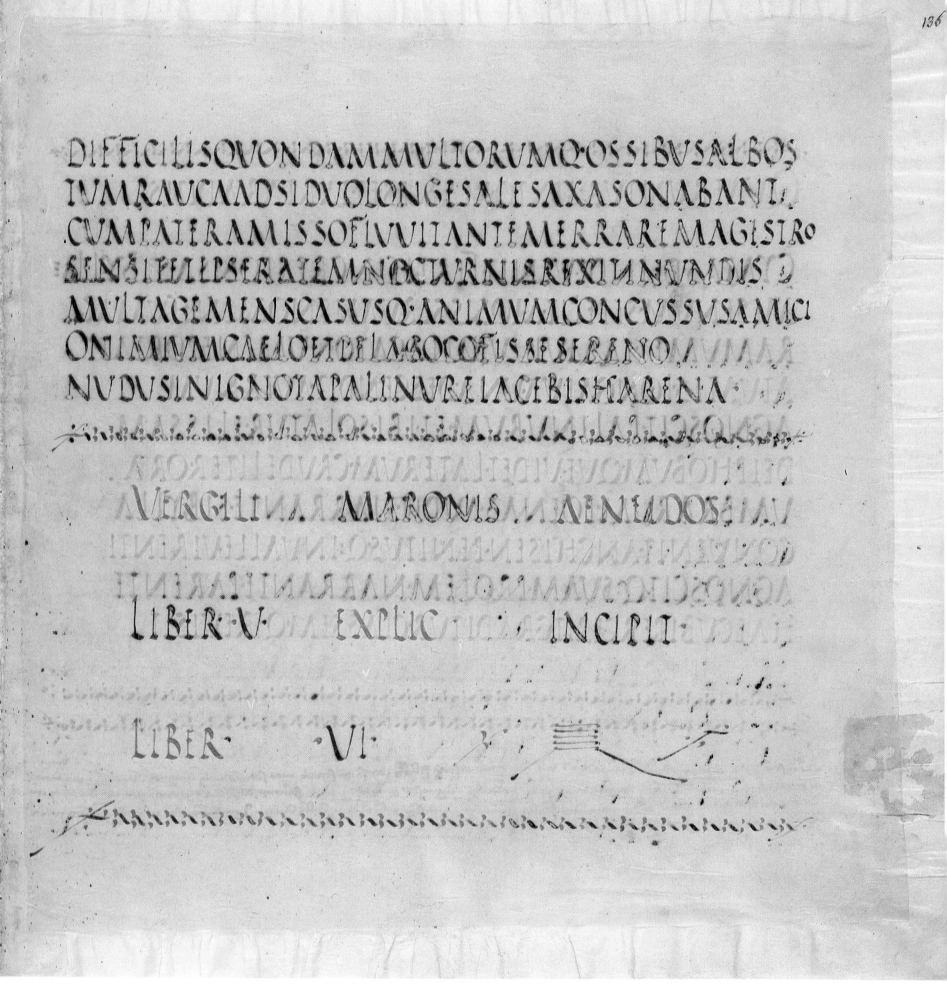

Final verses of *Aeneid* V and colophon (fol. 136r)

SEPTIMVS AENEAM REDDIT FATALIBVS ARVIS

HIC QVOQVE CALETAM SEPELIT TVM DEINDE PROFECTVS
LAVRENTVMQ· VENIT HANC VERBIS COGNOVIT IVLI
FATALEM TERRAM MENSIS ENVESCIMVR INQVIT
CENTVM ORATORES PACEM VENIAMQVE PETENTES
AD REGEM MITTVNT LAETITVM SORTE LATINVM
QVI CVM PACE ETIAM NATA CONVBIA PACTVS
HOC FORTE ALLECTO IVNONIS DISSIPATI RAM
CONCVRRVNT DICTIS QVAMVIS PIA FATA REPVGNENT
BELLI CAVSA FVIT VIOLATVS VVLNERE CERVVS
TVM GENTES SOCIAE ARMA PARANT FREMIT ARMA IVVENTVS

Summary of *Aeneid* VII (fol. 162v)

37

Iris Comes to Turnus (*Aen.* 9.1–5, fol. 74v misbound)

The surviving illustration for Book IX is the left half of the original pair; it shows the opening episode, where on instructions from Juno Iris comes to Turnus, the Rutulian Prince, as he is seated in a grove sacred to his ancestor Pilumnus, to tell him that Aeneas has left the Trojan camp to visit potential allies, and that this is the perfect time for him to attack. Turnus is seated, fully armed, but looks up and raises his right hand in a gesture of speech to respond to Iris (though in the text he speaks only after she has left) while Iris flies in holding a billowing scarf and speaking with her right hand. The posture of both figures is comprehensible if awkward; Iris's shoulders are seen frontally but her hips are seen partly from behind. The spaceless ground is strewn with out-of-scale vegetation and a quiver, in our artist's usual decorator's manner; the miniature building at the upper left is probably a shrine connected with this grove. But despite the clumsy details, it is clear that our artist has advanced enormously from his work in the *Eclogues*, especially in the colouristic effects here.

(*referring to the next pair of illustrations*) The pair of illustrations showing the Council of the Gods at the opening of Book X are the most remarkable example of our artist's originality. As usual, details are clumsily executed but the totality of the pair fully achieves its purpose. On the left page Jupiter is enthroned in the centre, turning his head slightly to the right to look at Juno, who raises her hand in a gesture of speech. Across from her Minerva is enthroned and looking at Juno; next to her Mercury stands, also turning to look at Juno, while between Jupiter and Juno Vulcan stands looking forward, but in a direction we should understand as towards Juno, since this is the moment of her long speech denigrating Aeneas (verses 63-95).

On the opposite page Neptune is enthroned in the middle, Diana at the left, while Apollo stands between them, and at the right both Venus standing and Mars enthroned raise their hands in softer gestures of speech; Venus had already spoken (verses 18-62) but Mars does not speak in this episode. All these gods look straight out of the page, but if we imagine closing the book we realize that then they complete a circular group and also look at Juno. We must assume that the model did not have two pages for this scene but showed all the gods in one group, probably in an extended semi-circle with relatively coherent spatial recession, a normal composition for a council. With remarkable ingenuity our artist rearranged them to make two corresponding groups for the two pages and despite his consistent denial of spatial depth in his individual compositions he thought enough in terms of sophisticated three-dimensional relations to make all the gods at the right of the open book look across to the page at the left (when the book is closed).

This arrangement has one further expressive effect: all the gods on the page at the right look straight out of the page at the beholder; the only other figures in this manuscript to do so are Vulcan on the page at the left here and the author of the second *Eclogue*. In the case of the author the effect is probably accidental, reflecting our artist's lack of experience, for the faces of the authors decorating the fourth and sixth *Eclogues* turn slightly aside. But by the time he painted these gods our artist knew what he was doing. The effect of this gaze is inescapable, and it makes this a kind of devotional image. Furthermore, at this time Christian art was beginning to develop devotional images with comparable expressive force, reaching initial maturity in the time of Justinian. To treat these images of pagan gods this way must have been deliberate. As in the insertion of figures of pseudo-imperial authority authorizing the pagan sacrifice in honour of Anchises we seem to find evidence that our patron was a pagan sympathizer.

Council of the Gods, left half (fol. 234v)

Council of the Gods, right half (fol. 235r)

Combat of Aeneas and Turnus (*Aen.* 12.704-707, etc, folio 188v misbound)

The only surviving illustration to Book XII, the left half of the original pair, shows the single combat of Aeneas and Turnus near the end of the book, but it is strangely confused and clumsy. At the left the Trojans stand watching (as specified in verses 704-7) as Aeneas draws his bow, but the text never has him use bow and arrow in this fight; at first both Aeneas and Turnus hurl their spears from some distance and then they fight with swords. To have Turnus at the right preparing to hurl a spear is therefore correct, but not at such close quarters. The anatomy of Aeneas stepping forward as he draws his bow is better than most such figures executed by our artist but is hardly rational, since standing still allows better aim for the arrow. The anatomy of Turnus, seen from behind, shows our artist's usual confusion. The basic arrangement of the two opposing groups squeezed into a square format leaves a flat empty area between them with only a quiver and three stray arrows for a partial strewn-ground effect.

We can imagine an iconographic model in more classical style, with the groups separated and distributed in a coherent landscape, but we would not expect a model from around the time of the Vatican Vergil to make the obvious mistake of showing Aeneas with bow and arrow. So we should consider how much of this illustration may have been improvised by our artist, as he improvised the bucolic scenes for *Eclogues* three, five and seven, and for *Georgics* Book III. The figure of Aeneas here could have been taken from his figure of Ascanius in Book V and given armour, as obviously necessary. Our artist may have taken figures from some other battle scene in his model, for which no copy survives in the Roman Vergil. But the standing soldiers here are notably less competently drawn than those in the scene of Sinon and Priam (p. 29) and so it seems more likely that our painter improvised the whole, drawing on stock figures of soldiers just as he drew on stock figures of shepherds in the *Eclogues*. Indeed, the awkward quality in every aspect of this miniature contrasts with our artist's relative competence in copying comparable scenes such as Ascanius Shooting the Stag and Iris coming to Turnus, and suggests that this miniature is entirely our artist's invention.

The older manuscript our artist used as his iconographic model for the *Aeneid* was probably defective at the end and our artist had to develop two new illustrations, this one for the single combat, which is narrated near the end of the Book (unlike the other left-hand miniatures referring to episodes at the beginning of a Book) and probably the death of Turnus for the lost right-hand part of the pair. Thus it seems that without a model from which to extract, he thought about the content of the Book as a whole and depicted the two most important moments in it, perhaps depending on his patron's advice.

Looking back now at his earlier work we can see that our painter has improved his technique, but when he must work without an iconographic model, we still find the same misunderstanding of anatomy, the same formulaic profile, and the same decorator's instinct for the spaceless strewn ground as in his early work. For greater legibility he had depended on a model in classical style, as in his first *Eclogue* illustration and in his other *Aeneid* illustrations.

As originally produced, the Roman Vergil was an enormous book of 410 folios measuring approximately 350 x 335 mm; after centuries of rough handling and repeated trimmings for rebinding now there are 309 folios of 335 x 325 mm or slightly smaller. The book was too big to hold for reading; it was made for display on a stand. Indeed, among surviving Late Antique literary manuscripts we have only fragments of one book significantly larger (the Augustan Vergil, of about 430 x 360 mm, see page 64) and fragments of two roughly the same size (Vergil in St Gallen and Lucan in Naples). The Vatican Vergil, on the other hand, was slightly longer (around 435 folios) but much smaller in page size (about 240 x 210 mm), a convenient size to hold for reading, though fairly heavy.

The parchment of the Roman Vergil is extraordinarily fine, very thin, originally very white on the flesh side and nearly as white on the hair side, and without any blemishes. The Vatican Vergil has similar parchment but not quite as fine, and several of its folios show original defects, even one page with a small hole within the written area. Unfortunately, the extreme fineness of membrane meant that the acid in the ink tended to eat through the skin, in some pages even causing the loss of small bits of parchment between letters. Therefore in a rebinding in 1867 thin paper was pasted down as protection on almost all the written pages, though not on any of the illustrations; the text pages reproduced here on pp. 36-7 are relatively well preserved, but do show some of the effects of deterioration and repair.

The manufacturing process began by assembling the skins from 205 sheep, soaking them in lye, a strong alkali that loosened the fat, scraping them thoroughly, stretching them to dry and then trimming them to size. The sheets were pricked so delicately that it is hard to find the marks, and then they were ruled with a stylus on every flesh side for eighteen lines of text, with vertical bounding lines defining a frame of 220 x 245 mm. The sheets were next collected and folded, apparently in sets of four (though no bifolium of text survives intact), with the hair side outside and flesh facing flesh, hair facing hair throughout the text, as expected in fine books. This matching was done because the flesh side can be a little whiter even in this very fine parchment. The pairs of illustrations were executed separately on sheets that had not been ruled for text, painted always on the flesh side, and later inserted into the gatherings of text even when that meant interrupting the sequence of openings with

like facings; clearly the idea of displaying a pair of frontispiece illustrations took priority over the normal arrangement of flesh and hair sides.

The text was written in the enamel-like brown ink normal in Late Antique books, using a reed pen trimmed to produce at will either very broad lines or very fine hair-lines. The effect of this strong shading is obvious in the letters O and Q, where the axis of round strokes can be seen to be about 60° (that is, tilted about 30° to the left of vertical); this is also approximately the axis of the broad diagonal strokes in N, R, and X (the detail in p. 45 is enlarged two times). Some rather elaborate letters are easily understood as being formed by a natural series of rhythmic strokes made with the pen held consistently at the same angle, S for example, or G (always in the capital form), but there is an obvious exception in the thin strokes of A, M, and U, which are generally no more than a hair-line.

To produce these letters the scribe first drew the heavy stroke down and to the right, at an axis of about 70°, with a slight upward flip at the end; then he lifted his pen, rotated it to the left, and drew the hairline down and to the left, at an axis of about 10° (that is, 80° down from the vertical). At the end of that stroke, perhaps without lifting his pen but moving it back very slightly, he pulled the pen towards him at the same low angle to make the club-footed serif. There is the strongest possible contrast here between thick and thin strokes, but the two types of stroke are far from being at right angles to each other, as they would be in a simple natural motion. The M is particularly complex: first the scribe drew his usual A (compare the last two letters in the second line on p. 45); then he drew the heavy descender at the right at a slightly more vertical angle, and finally the hair-line down from near the top of that stroke to meet the previous heavy line. This sequence is proven by the occasional blotting of ink from the second heavy stroke (then still wet) into the top of the hair-line and by the very rare example at the bottom of the illustration on p. 45 where the hair-line misses the first heavy stroke.

In fact, the scribe was constantly adjusting his angle of approach, for simple vertical strokes (as in I and L) are narrower than they would be if drawn at the same angle as O and Q, and the vertical strokes of N are generally slightly thinner than those of I and L. Correspondingly, many broad strokes are wider than they would be if made at the basic angle, especially the club-foot-

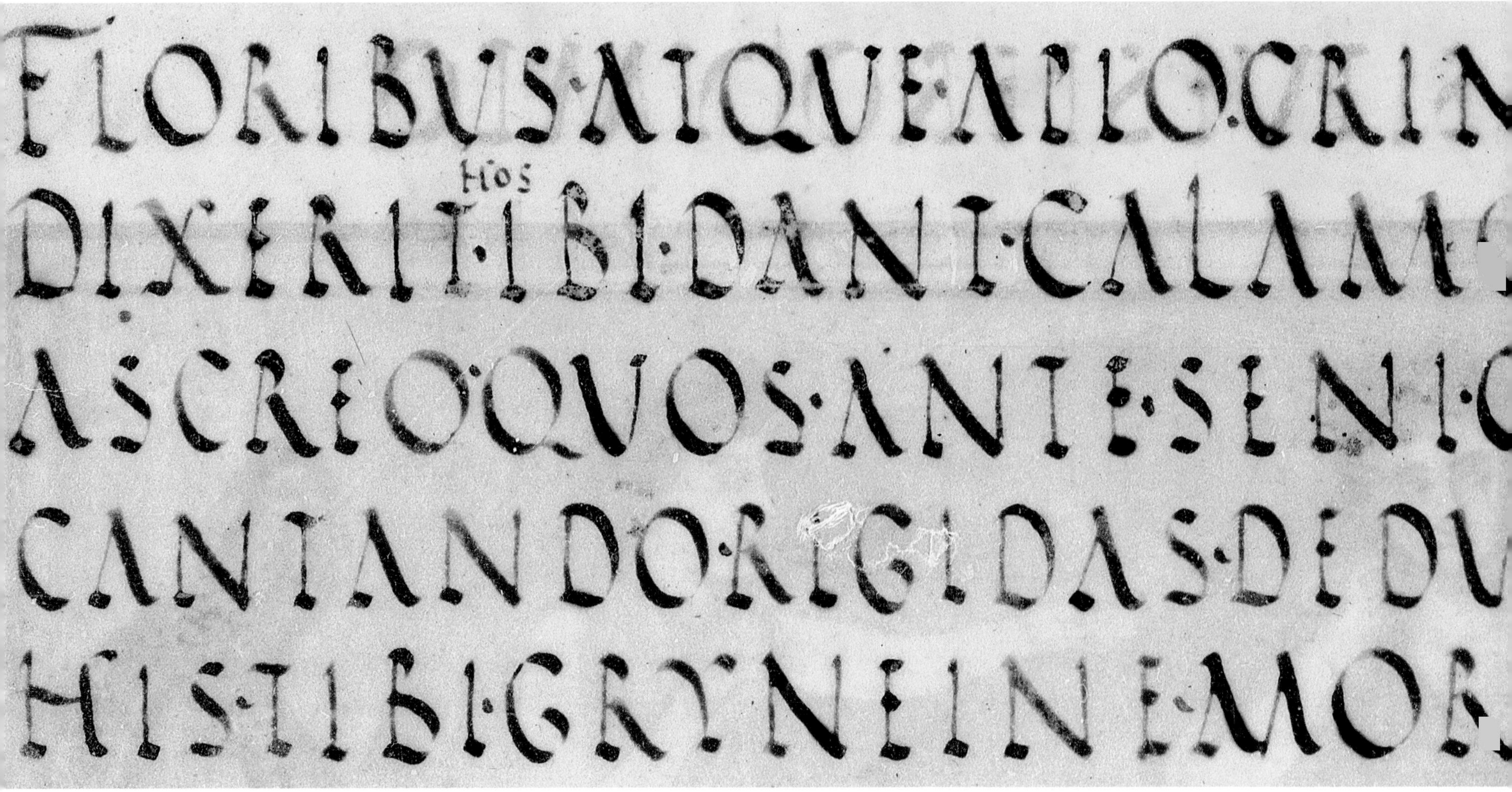

FLORIBVS·ATQVE·APIO·CRIN
hos
DIXERIT·TIBI·DANT·CALAM
ASCRÆOQVOS·ANTE·SENIC
CANTANDO·RIGIDAS·DEDV
HIS·TIBI·GRYNEINEMO

Detail of script twice actual size (fol. 16r, *Ecl.* 6.68-72)

ed serifs at the bottom of many vertical strokes (as E, F, I, R, T), which require a very low angle, about 10°, the same as that used for the hair-line strokes in A, M, and U.

This is a very elaborate version of the standard capital script of Rome, often today known as Rustic capitals to distinguish it from the very formal Square capitals of grand inscriptions, as on the Column of Trajan. Although primarily suited to the pen, Rustic capitals are found, for example, in the poster announcements drawn on the walls of Pompeii and became common in less important inscriptions, their epigraphic form being known as *scriptura actuaria*. The letter forms in the Roman Vergil are generally standard but one of the letters has a highly man-

nered late form: the H looks like an I followed by a compressed C with a connecting stroke between them. It was formed in five strokes: first a narrow descender, then (perhaps without lifting the pen) a club-footed serif, next the separate horizontal stroke shaped almost like a tilde, then the broad vertical descender curving slightly at the bottom, and finally the downward hook to the right at the top. The first two strokes were made at an angle of about 15°, the third (the tilde) at a slightly higher angle, and the last two were made at an angle of about 80°. Even when this scribe returned to write a correction with a narrow pen in very small script (above) he followed the same form but with less careful detailing.

SAECVLI NOVI INTERPRAEFATIO

POE SICELIDESMVSAEPAVLOMAIORACANAMVS

NONOMNESARBVSTAIVVANTHVMILESQ·MYRICA

SICANIBVSSILVASSILVAESINTCONSVLEDIGNAE

Top and bottom lines of fol. 9v actual size (*Ecl.* 4.1-2, 4.16-17)

ILLEDEVMVITAMACCIPIETDIVISQVEVIDEBIT

PERMIXTOSHEROASETIPSEVIDEBITVRILLIS

PACATVMQ·REGETPATRIISVIRTVTIBVSORBEM

Other features contribute to the decorative effect of this script: B, F, and L regularly rise slightly above the top of the line of script; the top stroke of F often takes the form of an extended flourish and the bottom stroke of L or the tail of Q may be given similar treatment at the bottom of a page (see above). The first letter on a page is usually slightly larger, especially so when it is a title (above). When crowded at the end of a line the scribe will compress his script to avoid disrupting the format of the page. The astonishing fact is that this scribe was absolutely consistent in drawing these very elaborate letters, always closely and evenly spaced in *scriptura continua*, throughout nearly 800 pages of copying. (Incidentally, in examining these reproductions of the script it is important to realize that the points inserted to separate words are an addition by a later ancient corrector.)

The Vatican Vergil, on the other hand, has letters only about half as tall, with squarer proportions, spaced more openly along the line, and formed with more natural motions of the hand, without such large changes in the angle of approach (see detail on facing page, enlarged two times). The broad strokes are comparably broad but there are few hair-line strokes and the serifs are less prominent; furthermore the H has the traditional nearly square shape made in three strokes. The Vatican Vergil script has great dignity of effect but none of the elegance of what is actually a very mannered script in the Roman Vergil, which has a formal character we might think suitable for engraving on stone, although the shape of the club-footed serifs is geared to penmanship. That formality is even more evident in the other two enormous Vergil manuscripts, the Vergilius

Augusteus (see p. 65) and the St Gallen fragments, which are actually written in Square capitals, the script of grand imperial inscriptions, as carved on the Column of Trajan, or made of bronze and set into marble on the Arch of Constantine. The Roman Vergil is extraordinarily elegant but its script remains a book hand rather than an imitation of monumental inscriptions.

The text of our manuscript is basically good, despite what seems to be its incorporation of some Late Antique glosses, but it is carelessly copied, with some eccentric spelling, and it often omits short syllables when the same two or three letters occur at the end of one word and at the beginning of the next. There are normally no abbreviations (except the suspensions B· for -*bus* and Q· for -*que* when crowded at the end of a line) but there is one interesting exception: of the 43 occurrences of the word *deus* three use the abbreviation $\overline{\text{DS}}$. This was the normal usage for *nomina sacra* in Christian texts, both biblical and patristic, but not in classical literature; this seems to indicate that our scribe had been employed in copying Christian texts and forgot himself on these three isolated occasions.

The chronological sequence here of the three authentic works of Vergil is standard but there are some innovations in the accessories. There are titles in red above *Eclogues* 2-6 (see illustrations on pp. 16, 17, 20, and above) that also occur in the Vergilius Palatinus, a fine unillustrated manuscript about a generation older, but they appear to be a Late Antique invention. The Roman Vergil is the only ancient manuscript of Vergil with the prefatory poems that became common in the Carolingian era. Before each book of the *Georgics* there is a poem of four verses on a separate page and before each book of the *Aeneid* there is both a single verse characterizing the book and a poem of ten verses summarizing it (see example illustrated on p. 37). These are characteristic of Late Antique scholarship but their origin is not known.

The illustrations for the *Eclogues* were planned by the scribe when he left space for them before each of the separate poems, and could only be executed after he had finished writing. The first time he left the top nine lines (half the page) empty; the second time he left eleven lines empty in the middle of the page, but for some reason he left only eight lines empty at the top of the page for the third *Eclogue* and since after the first *Eclogue* our artist always made frames for his illustrations the result is very crowded (see p. 17). Even worse, for the fourth *Eclogue* the artist had to make do with only six lines at the bottom of the page, on the page before the poem began (p. 18); a more generous scribe would have considered those six lines wasted and would have left the upper half of the following page empty for this illustration. For the fifth *Eclogue* the artist had eight lines empty at the bottom of a page, for the sixth he had nine lines empty in the middle of the page after one isolated last line of the previous *Eclogue* (which the scribe chose not to put in the bottom margin of the previous page), and for the seventh he had eleven lines at the bottom of a page. Clearly the *Eclogues* were not considered important enough to deserve a proper headpiece illustration, always at the top of a page, for which purpose empty space might have to be left at the end of the previous poem. Even failing that, since the number of verses in each poem is easily counted and the text pages always have eighteen lines, the scribe could easily have done a better job of planning these smaller illustrations; he was of course copying from an unillustrated exemplar and the irregularity of spacing here suggests that he was not accustomed to producing illustrated books.

The major illustrations, always a pair of facing frames roughly the same size as the area of written text, were an entirely separate campaign, executed on separate bifolia of the same very fine parchment, without any ruling, left blank on the first recto and the second verso to enhance the dignity of this display. They were painted always on the flesh side, which is slightly whiter, with a normal range of mineral and organic pigments and with applications of gold leaf and a few details in granulated silver (in the spear tips of the witnesses to the Sacrifice in Honour of Anchises, see p. 32). The colours were applied with some blending, which was the old classical tradition, but also relied sometimes on a succession of thin washes, a technique not used in the Vatican Vergil. The painter's first work (p. 15) is so clumsy, especially in the heavy contour of the left leg of the standing Meliboeus, that it seems this craftsman cannot have been accustomed to painting miniatures in a book, but his technique improved in the next pages and by Book IV of the *Aeneid* his choice of iconography has become more sophisticated (see p. 48).

Detail of Vatican Vergil script twice actual size (*Aen.* 4.670, 678-680, fol. 41v)

The illustration to the first *Eclogue* (p. 15) must have been copied from an authentic model; certainly a painter who would produce such a mess the next time he made a comparable illustration (p. 17), improvising from his repertory of standard motifs, could not have invented from scratch a miniature that so convincingly illustrates the text, that despite its very clumsy draftsmanship accurately shows correct details of dress and reasonable articulation of anatomy. The lack of frame and painted background, features found in all the other miniatures in this book, suggests that the model might have been quite early; this is the "papyrus style" and it is reasonable to suppose that an illustration to go at the beginning of a roll with the work of the great national poet might have been created early in the flourishing of Roman culture and might have started a tradition for this illustration. There is a closely related Carolingian drawing and two more distant Italian reflections of such an iconography but we have no way of arguing a specific date for the origin of this composition or for the date of the exemplar our artist copied. That could have been a considerably older papyrus roll or it could have been a faithful copy of such a roll in a codex made around the time of the Vatican Vergil, but not the one that supplied models for our *Aeneid* illustrations, where the illustrations certainly had painted backgrounds and frames. Not all codices in that era used frames and painted backgrounds; the lost Late Antique illustrated Terence (known from Carolingian copies) did not have them for its 147 completely original and highly expressive narrative illustrations.

The *Aeneid* illustrations in our book (except for the last one) were certainly copied, with some modifications, from a codex with accurate narrative illustrations. Our first surviving *Aeneid* illustration, the Storm at Sea (p. 25), when examined with tolerant eyes, clearly suggests the style of the exemplar. If we imagine improving the details of figure style and of painting technique, and eliminating the intrusive sea monsters at the bottom of the composition, we can imagine an illustration comparable to the best of the seascapes in the Vatican Vergil (facing page). In this illustration of the start of the ship race in Book V we have an open vista with deep recession clearly established by striations of colour on the plane of the sea and by colouristic distinctions at the distant horizon; that is what is clumsily copied in our book. Similarly, the scene of Aeneas and the Sibyl sacrificing before entering the underworld (facing page) is set in a deep landscape and suggests some of the features that must have been in the model of the Roman Vergil before the artist changed the

iconography of the Sacrifice in Honour of Anchises by inserting the three figures who preside over it (p. 32). The scene of Messapus Supervising the Siege of the Trojan Camp in the Vatican Vergil (p. 51) shows the same repertory of motifs and the same disparity of scale between people and fortification as in our scene of Sinon and Priam (p. 29). On the basis of these comparisons it is easy to imagine iconographic models for our *Aeneid* illustrations in the style of the Vatican Vergil and we should assume that they had a horizontal format, as normal there, since our illustrations could easily be rearranged in a horizontal frame; Dido's Banquet, for example, is intrinsically a horizontal shape and Ascanius Shooting the Stag would be much more comprehensible if rearranged in that format.

We can also assume that our artist extracted illustrations from their proper place in the text, just before the verses that narrate the episode, and it seems he tended to take the first two illustrations he found suitable in each book. Dido's Banquet, Iris Coming to Turnus, and the Council of the Gods all illustrate specifically the opening verses of their books, and the Sacrifice in Honour of Anchises is the most important phase of the first episode in its book. To consider cases where the second half of the pair of frontispieces survives, the Storm at Sea was clearly the second possible illustration in Book I and Priam and Sinon probably the second in Book II (but possibly the third); in these cases it does seem our artist simply copied the first two miniatures in his exemplar. But later he seems to have paid more attention to the selecting process and to have chosen illustrations that come towards the middle of the book but are appropriate as frontispieces because they are turning points in the story: Dido and Aeneas in the Cave, and Ascanius Shooting the Stag. The last miniature, Aeneas and Turnus in Single Combat, is so inaccurate in terms of the text and so clumsy in execution that it must have been improvised by our painter, just as he invented all the illustrations for the *Eclogues* except the first and all for the *Georgics*. In those books his exemplar must have had no illustrations; most likely it was also defective at the end of the *Aeneid* and our artist was forced to improvise. The battle scene illustrates in general the last episode in Book XII but it was the left half of a pair and presumably was matched with the scene where Aeneas kills the wounded Turnus with his sword, in the final verses of the epic; this was an intelligent choice by our artist, to select first the start of the key event and then the climactic moment of the book, even if the result was a sadly inept illustration.

Vatican Vergil: Start of the Ship Race (*Aen.* 5.114–138, fol.42r, actual size)

Vatican Vergil: Aeneas and the Sibyl Sacrificing (*Aen.* 6.45–46, fol. 46v, actual size)

49

The exemplar we postulate must have been in codex form, since clearly it had illustrations with frames and painted backgrounds that would have been impractical in a roll; therefore it is very unlikely to have been made before the fourth century, when the codex became the normal form for classical literature (although Christian writings began to appear in codex form in the second century), and the style needed to account for the seascape in the Storm at Sea points to the time around the year 400, the approximate date of the Vatican Vergil. The exemplar cannot have been the Vatican Vergil itself because it has a full series of illustrations for the *Georgics* and presumably had a series also for the *Eclogues*, which our artist surely would have used if they had been available. Furthermore, as these two incomplete manuscripts survive they never illustrate the same episode in the *Aeneid*. But since the *Aeneid* illustrations in the Vatican Vergil must have been adapted from an exemplar in papyrus style, most likely a set of older rolls, the question arises whether that "father" of the Vatican Vergil could have been the "grandfather" of the Roman Vergil or whether the ancestry of the Roman Vergil should be traced to a different early cycle of *Aeneid* illustrations.

There is one episode for which illustrations in these two books come very close together in the text, Ascanius Shooting the Stag in the Roman Vergil (p. 35) and the Wounded Stag Returning to Silvia in the Vatican Vergil (p. 51). In the Vatican Vergil the shooting episode would have come above verse 493 or perhaps verse 496, a part of the text that survives in the manuscript without any illustration, and the Return of the Stag comes above verse 503. Furthermore traces of a lost painting show that the Vatican Vergil had another illustration above verse 483, where the stag is first mentioned, an illustration presumably showing it kept as a pet in the family of Tyrrhus. That means there were paintings only twenty verses apart, which is unusually close for this manuscript. If we imagine an ancestor including the two known illustrations in the Vatican Vergil and the one in the Roman Vergil we are postulating a roll with paintings only ten verses apart, an arrangement quite unprecedented and most unlikely. Therefore it seems the ancestry of the cycle of illustrations from which those in the Roman Vergil were selected for copying was separate from the ancestry of the Vatican Vergil, that therefore there were actually two full sets of *Aeneid* illustrations in circulation in Late Antiquity.

We have little evidence to determine the origin of these cycles though it is easy to understand how once such a full series of illustrations to the *Aeneid* was created a scriptorium producing rolls of the *Aeneid* would prefer to copy from a master set of illustrations rather than reinvent something close to three hundred illustrations; therefore such a cycle could live on for many generations. For the Vatican Vergil there is evidence for the date of the prototype in details of military dress that closely match the Column of Trajan and disappear before the end of the second century; furthermore the task of fully illustrating the *Aeneid* would be compa-

rable to the achievement of designing the frieze on the Column, and the figure style we expect in the model for the Vatican Vergil illustrations would be at home in the Trajanic era. On the other hand, corresponding details in the Roman Vergil, such as leggings and tunics with sleeves, are specific to Late Antiquity; but they might be the contribution of our artist and may not be evidence for dating his exemplar.

In general there is suprisingly little sign of early illustration for the *Aeneid*, especially in view of its immediate popularity. The familiar formula of Aeneas carrying Anchises on his shoulder and leading Ascanius out of Troy does not count, for it goes back to Greek vases of the fifth century B.C. and was popularized on the coins of Julius Caesar. Two frescoes in Pompeii clearly depend on the same model for their depiction of the death of Laocoön and follow the text rather closely (but differ significantly from the illustration in the Vatican Vergil), and another fresco in Pompeii follows the text even more closely in showing Venus arriving to help Iapyx heal Aeneas's wound (12.383-440) but these frescoes must be seen in their context of luxurious wall decoration in the middle of the first century A.D., depicting various mythological subjects selected from a painter's notebook. Two instances like this do not justify reconstructing a full series of illustrations of Vergil's works in early rolls.

For the *Georgics*, on the other hand, it seems there never was an established set of illustrations in circulation. The surviving pair in the Roman Vergil is obviously an improvisation by our artist and the nine *Georgics* illustrations that survive in the Vatican Vergil give various signs of being invented on the spot. The Old Corycian (p. 54), for example, is shown seated on a rock explaining to two peasants the joy he takes in his flowers and fruits and in the honey the bees provide (*Georg.* 4.125-46). They approach with their hands out and palm up to indicate their acceptance of what he says, while at the right another man in workman's dress also speaks with his right hand raised but less emphatically; he is a stand-in for the poet, who writes specifically that he had met this old man near Taranto on the heel of Italy. Vergil describes specifically the rocky bit of land the man lives on as unfit for sheep or vines, but that is not at all what is shown in the miniature, with its open field and formulaic palace instead of the modest hut implicit in Vergil's story. Here we find improvisation using stock motifs vastly more capably than in the work of our artist and we observe a specifically Late Antique attitude in adding the figure of a commentator, a striking invention typical of the flourishing antiquarian culture of the beginning of the fifth century.

Pastoral scenes had been prominent in Roman art ever since the sacro-idyllic landscapes of the Augustan period and therefore even a decorator of modest ability like our painter knew the repertory. The Old Corycian in the Vatican Vergil shows a little of that repertory, and the mosaic in S. Maria Maggiore depicting the Calling of Moses is a much more convincing adaptation of a traditional bucolic scene (p. 55). A large

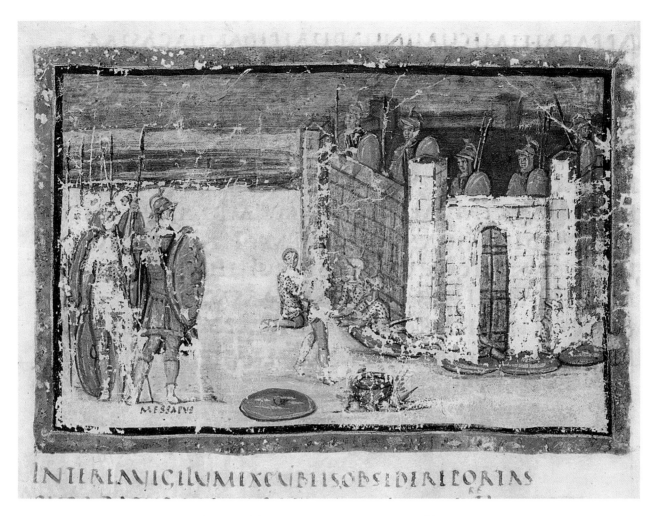

Vatican Vergil: Siege of the Trojan Camp (*Aen.* 9.159-169, fol. 72v, actual size)

Vatican Vergil: Silvia's Wounded Stag Returns and War Breaks Out (*Aen.* 7.500-537, fol. 66v, actual size)

Pastoral sarcophagus at the Isola Sacra near Ostia, c. 300

sarcophagus in the Isola Sacra cemetery near Ostia (above), from around 300, shows some more variations on these motifs. It has a standing figure leaning on his staff and resting his head on his hand much like the one here in *Georgics* Book III (p. 22) and it is carved in a crude style making a better comparison for our painter's work than the elegant painting of the Vatican Vergil.

Another aspect of standard repertory that our painter drew upon is the frontal image of a seated author holding a scroll. The statue of Poseidippus (at the right), a Roman adaptation of a Hellenistic portrait, gives a good idea of the basic type and shows rational draping of the cloak. Our artist's first version (p. 16) is hopelessly wrong in doubling the edge of the cloak that emerges from under his left arm but his other two surviving versions are acceptable in this regard and to achieve this second arrangement Poseidippus would only need to draw the hanging end further across his lap so that it hung outside his right leg. The formula used here originated in statuary but had been adapted for painting at least since the early third-century mosaic pavement from Sousse depicting Vergil flanked by two muses (but that particular pseudo-portrait bears no resemblance to this one). Another tradition implicit in a ghostly offset of a lost miniature in the Vatican Vergil was to place a bust of the author in a medallion, and this may have been a common practice in rolls, but it did not influence our artist.

Another Hellenistic tradition upon which our artist drew, in its common Roman form, was the decorator's illusionistic trick of the "unswept floor", a scattering of foliage and miscellaneous objects on a white background. A pair of mosaic panels in

Statue of the author Poseidippus, Roman adaptation of a Hellenistic statue (Vatican Museum)

the annular vault of the Constantinian mausoleum in Rome, now known as S. Costanza (below, left), is a good example from the middle of the fourth century. It shows the attitude that led to the strewn foliage in the *Georgics* illustrations (pp. 22-3) and also in several of the *Aeneid* illustrations, including the displaced quivers in the scenes with Iris and Turnus and with Aeneas and Turnus (pp. 38, 42). One other borrowed motif is specific to late Roman imperial art, the group of three presiding Trojans in the Sacrifice in Honour of Anchises (p. 32). The enormous gold medallion of Valens, showing him with his brother Valentinian I (below, right), struck in Rome between 364 and 367, is a particular-

ly good example for us because it includes palm leaves and bags of coins as prizes. Two details here, the high-backed throne and the nimbus, are restricted to emperors, but this general scheme was common in the fifth century for Consuls and other patrons presiding over the games, and in miniature the scheme appeared occasionally on imperial gold coinage throughout the fifth century, especially when the Emperor was to be shown as Consul. No wealthy art patron in the fifth century could have missed the symbolic connection and therefore we must interpret this intrusion into the narrative as in some way a deliberate statement favouring the pagan tradition.

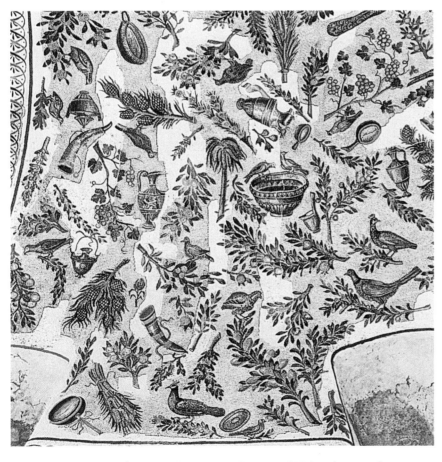

Vault mosaic, S. Costanza, Rome, c. 360 (much restored)

Gold medallion of Valens, with Valentian, 364–367 (Vienna, 1.5 x actual size)

53

For the study of painting in Rome during the fifth century we have only one dated monument with compositions comparable to ours: the mosaics of Old Testament subjects along the nave walls of S. Maria Maggiore, made for Sixtus III between 432 and 440. These, however, reveal such different directions of stylistic development that they require especially careful consideration. The depiction of the Calling of Moses, for example (facing page), is a very successful copy of a traditional bucolic scene with slight modifications introduced to make the central shepherd look up to the right to see the inserted Hand of God, while reaching out with his right palm up to show that he is receiving the Word of God. The burning bush and the action of Moses turning aside to see this strange phenomenon, as specified in the text (Ex. 3.2-3), is less important theologically than the receiving of the Word and therefore can be omitted for convenience in adapting a fine secular model. So when we find well-coordinated turning motions in the figures, and both men and sheep convincingly located in a continuously receding landscape, we must attribute these qualities not to fifth-century style but to the skill of this mosaicist in copying a much older model, perhaps from the second century. This phenomenon is comparable to our illustration of the Storm at Sea (p. 25) but much better executed.

Vatican Vergil: The Old Corycian Explains his Simple Life (*Georg.* 4.125-146, fol. 7*v*, actual size)

It is useful to compare this mosaic with the illustration of the Old Corycian in the Vatican Vergil (facing page) for although those figures are coherently three-dimensional, they do not turn freely in space and they are all aligned on the same strip of ground, which seems to be the near edge of a flower bed (vaguely implicit in the text). There is no trackable continuity in the landscape beyond the shallow foreground group until we come to the distant formulaic palace and the woods behind it; this and the mindless duplication of two identical workers stepping forward with open hands to receive the words of the Corycian are clear symptoms of improvisation; this artist in the Vatican Vergil was a very skilful painter but he had only limited capacity to invent compositions in classical style. If we take the S. Maria Maggiore mosaic not as a work of 432–40 but as an accurate copy of a very much older bucolic painting, this comparison allows us to see the Old Corycian as a worthy invention around 400 that satisfies the need to illustrate the text but betrays Late Antique qualities in composition. In contrast, our painter's work in improvising illustrations for similar subjects is not merely clumsy in technique but reveals a fundamental loss of understanding of anatomy and of the articulation of drapery, and in his *Georgics* illustrations (pp. 22–3) he suppresses entirely the idea of spatial continuity.

S. Maria Maggiore: The Calling of Moses (432–440)

The mosaic of the Separation of Lot and Abram (facing page), on the other hand, is one of the least classical — in that sense one of the most advanced — examples of style in the church. The chief protagonists are pressed forward toward the picture plane and treated as voluminous and substantial, very plastic, while the figures behind them are no more than cardboard cutouts, clustered together as two spaceless groups. The articulation of Abram is satisfactory but there are problems with the legs and hips of Lot, and the damaged figures of shepherds below are flat and turn their heads up in a very awkward way, entirely unlike the plastically treated shepherds turning freely in space in the Calling of Moses. Looking back to the dated sequence of ivories we have studied (pp. 8-12) we can find a similar quality of shallowness and lack of substance in the diptych of Felix in 428, roughly a decade earlier.

The spatial configuration in Lot and Abram is the extreme opposite of that in the Calling of Moses, for in the pastoral scene at the bottom of the mosaic the various animals and plants are separate units scattered on a spaceless gold background without any major overlapping, thus approaching our painter's *Georgics* compositions (pp. 22-3). The clustering of Abram and his followers and of Lot and his followers is enhanced by separating them by a narrow strip of gold background that reaches almost to their feet and reinforces the idea of separation that is basic for the incident (Gen. 13.8-12); this is clearly an initial step in the direction of the Single Combat between Aeneas and Turnus (p. 42) which our artist improvised out of his repertory of figures. Even making due allowance for the clumsy draftsmanship of our painter it is clear that his battle scene must be considerably later than the mosaics of S. Maria Maggiore.

Another of these mosaics is particularly interesting for its spatial composition and reinforces this conclusion. The composition of the Crossing of the Red Sea (p. 59) is obviously the result of compressing a long horizontal composition into a square to fit the format of this panel, resulting in a V-shaped arrangement of the main elements and placing the figure of the drowning Pharaoh near the top, evidently in the distance. The same compression from the sides produced our painter's Ascanius Shooting the Stag (p. 35) but that is much more advanced in the spaceless effect, with its unmodulated flat ground filling the frame, while at S. Maria Maggiore there is both a receding shoreline and a horizon to establish at least the ghost of a coherent space. By comparison, the scene in the Vatican Vergil of Aeneas and Achates Finding Carthage under Construction (p. 58) is a much less disturbing example of compressing a horizontal composition into a square. The various episodes of quarrying and construction each take place in an established space and they are scattered within the square shape with reasonable coherence, including colour gradations to establish space between the city and the hill where Aeneas and Achates are standing. Even though this miniature is by the worst of the three hands in the Vatican Vergil we do find here an intuitive sense of spatial composition that dwindles away during the rest of the century. The overall flatness of the scene of Dido and Aeneas in the Cave will come at the end of a long evolution.

To return to the sequence of ivory carvings, the strange compression and distortion in the upper body of the *divus* being carried aloft in the Apotheosis panel (p. 10) is clearly a step in the direction of our painter's figures, though there is no exact comparison. Much closer is the ivory of Basilius (p. 11), Consul in 480, where the distortions in the anatomy of the victory closely resemble the work of our painter; the drapery over her legs is particularly close to that of his third author portrait (p. 20) and of the presiding figures in the Sacrifice in Honour of Anchises (p. 32). The Consular diptych of Boethius (p. 12) is a still closer comparison in its general suppression of anatomy, and its harsh distortions of the face are analogous to the formulaic faces in our painter's work, though the formula is not the same.

S. Maria Maggiore: The Separation of Lot and Abram (432–440)

Vatican Vergil: Aeneas and Achates Find Carthage under Construction (*Aen.* 1.418–429, folio 13r, actual size)

S. Maria Maggiore: Crossing the Red Sea (432–440)

On the other hand the style of our paintings cannot be assigned to the sixth century, when a renewed plasticity developed in figures, but without the full anatomical coordination of the older classical tradition. The beginning of this development is evident in the mosaics of the Arian Baptistery in Ravenna, where there are two successive phases of work dating from the years around 500. The first campaign executed the Baptism at the top of the vault and the figures of Peter, Paul, and another apostle at the left approaching the altar; the second campaign executed the rest of the apostles. The figure of St Peter (below) is very flat, his face crudely rendered and his drapery stiffly linear, while St Andrew following him at the right is far more plastic and voluminous, his head more convincing. His bent left leg is clearly articulated and both it and his shoulders have shading along the back contour to establish their volume; the main diagonal folds passing over his body almost seem to be tubular. The figure following St Andrew is similar. This is the style of the second crew of mosaicists, who are beginning to develop what will become the Justinianic style, which in these same years is particularly clear in the standing figures on the walls of S. Apollinare Nuovo. There is no hint of that style in the work of our painter, who must therefore have worked a little earlier, probably in the 480s.

Ravenna, Arian Baptistery, detail of Apostles (c. 500)

The date of the Roman Vergil is established primarily by the figure style and the spatial composition of the illustrations. In both aspects our painter's work clearly comes well after the period of classical revival around 400 but has none of the positive features of the future Justinianic style. The dated ivory carvings of Basilius (480) and Boethius (487) are particularly close to our painter's work, and the general suppression of spatial depth, even its complete elimination in the scene of Ascanius Shooting the Stag, go far beyond the most radical mosaics in S. Maria Maggiore (432–440).

On the other hand, our painter's work resembles somewhat the earlier campaign of mosaic decoration in the Arian Baptistery at Ravenna but is clearly different from the work of the second campaign there and from the first maturity of this style, as seen in the mosaics of S. Apollinare Nuovo early in the sixth century.

There figures are treated as very plastic in certain aspects but they do not move freely in space and they are often subject to restraints and to exaggeration in action for expressive purposes. This is particularly clear in a mosaic like the Multiplication of Loaves and Fishes (below), where the spatial composition is a tightly compressed sequence of layers from which Christ advances as a dominant image. In his treatment of the Council of the Gods our artist took some steps in that direction, and towards a composition like the enthroned Christ flanked by angels at S. Apollinare Nuovo, but he never achieved that spatial sophistication or expressive force (which in Ravenna is only a provincial reflection of the rising new art in Constantinople). Much less did he approach the grandeur and sophistication of the apse of SS. Cosma e Damiano in Rome (526–30).

Ravenna, S. Apollinare Nuovo: The Multiplication of Loaves and Fishes (early sixth century)

Therefore a date of around the 480s is indicated. Of course precision is not possible in an argument like this, but if we stick to convenient round numbers, it seems unlikely that the Roman Vergil was produced before about 470 or after about 500. Other aspects of the book are concordant with this conclusion. Rustic capital script is too rare and there are too few dated examples to permit any firm chronology but our extraordinarily large and elaborate version of the script must be generally late, especially with its special form of H, and therefore is likely to date from the second half of the fifth century. The occasional use of the Christian abbreviation for *deus* is also a late symptom but it need not require specifically a date in the sixth century, as has been suggested.

The attribution of the Roman Vergil to Rome rests largely on the standards of book production obvious in it, and the lack of reasonable alternatives in the last third of the fifth century. Size, parchment, and calligraphy are of superlatively high quality and Rome is the only centre likely to have had such possibilities at this time. There is no sign that Ravenna ever produced books of this character, especially not of classical literature. The only truly sumptuous work attributed to Ravenna is the unillustrated purple Gothic Gospels assumed to have been produced under Theoderic (493-526), which are written in silver on parchment dyed purple, reflecting Greek practices, and offering no point of comparison. Some art historians have preferred Ravenna for the Roman Vergil, apparently dazzled by the number of mosaics that happen to survive there, but in our period it was an isolated backwater under the Germanic general Odoacer. By the last part of the fifth century Milan can be ruled out and no other city could even be considered.

The conclusion is inevitable that the Roman workshop that produced the Roman Vergil had the highest possible standards of manufacture and of calligraphy, but did not have on its regular staff a painter of comparable merit. Indeed, in Rome at this time we know no trace of painting of appropriate quality. Clearly the patron insisted on illustrations and we may suppose the owner of this shop looked long and hard but could find no one skilled at painting in books. Our painter's first work is so incompetent in basic handling of the brush that we can assume he had never worked at this scale, but we have seen that gradually as he worked on successive miniatures he raised his technique to a respectable level. He may have worked previously at painting large panels or perhaps walls and he did have good control over mixing his pigments and binder.

He also had a taste for bright colours; the pigments are probably the same as in the Vatican Vergil but our artist tends to use them in larger areas, without gradations or shading (as in the Council of the Gods, pp. 40-1), often juxtaposing contrasting hues at high saturation (as in the area around Priam, p. 29). In the classical tradition of the Vatican Vergil blended gradations of colour are a basic technique and juxtapositions of different hues

are far more subdued. Our painter certainly has a decorator's instinct in choosing colours and in other aspects of composition, such as scattering foliage and other objects on the ground, as if this were an unswept-floor mosaic. The design on the sides of his framed incipit page is a normal decorator's motif, but he was not a very sophisticated decorator or he would have coordinated that design more tidily at the corners and flipped it over for symmetry. His decorator's taste is also evident in the way he takes care with certain details of dress, such as of Dido's jewelry at the banquet and the decorations on Priam's tunic (pp. 28-9).

He took care in painting details like that but was fundamentally incompetent in drawing the human figure. Even when we assume he had a good model he made a hopeless mess of the reclining Ascanius in the Banquet and distorted Aeneas's left arm terribly. Yet his distortions could also serve an expressive purpose, as in Priam's lengthened right arm when he speaks to Sinon; and the dislocations in the anatomy of Dido and Aeneas in the cave serve the narrative well. It must be his radical modifications of a model that make the Council of the Gods (pp. 40-1) so ingenious as a spatial composition of two facing pages that conceptually must be folded together, and his approach here to creating a devotional image is enhanced by the visionary effect of his decorative background of rainbow, sun, moon, and stars. Those motifs were probably in the model but the model must have been a single composition at the beginning of Book X, and it was our painter, perhaps with the advice of the patron, who created this powerful new image. We must acknowledge the negative aspects of our painter, considered from the point of view of the classical revival at the beginning of the fifth century, but we can find here the germ of new ideas that will develop with grand effect in the next generation, as at S. Apollinare Nuovo and SS. Cosma e Damiano.

The Roman Vergil is especially important as a turning point in the development of book design. The Vatican Vergil made the transition from roll to codex in a relatively straightforward manner; most of its illustrations retain the small horizontal format that fits comfortably in the correct place in the text, sometimes in the middle of a page. The new element there was the possibility of a painted background, including in the best painters' work deeply receding landscapes or seascapes (p. 49) or a fully organized interior space, in revived classical style, instead of the minimal group of figures and major objects that must have been shown in simplified papyrus style in the iconographic model for the *Aeneid*.

In the Vatican Vergil there had already appeared the first steps toward creating a more formal system of frontispiece illustration. The example that survives for Book III of the *Georgics* is a full page with six small scenes referring to the first dozen verses (which are written on the verso of this folio) and enclosed within a single frame, a feature obviously impossible in a roll and a unique invention for this codex, as far as we can see from surviving folios. A more elaborate system survives for Book III of the

Calendar of 354: Mars (copied 1620 from a Carolingian copy; Vatican, Barb. lat. 2154, fol. 9r)

Aeneid: there is a full-page illustration showing Aeneas setting sail from Troy (the opening episode) on the recto of a leaf that is left blank on the verso and the text begins with three lines in red on the next recto; but only twelve verses are needed to finish this episode, the rest of the page is left empty, and on the verso there is another full page-illustration for the second episode while the text for that one is on the facing recto of this planned sequence of illustrations resembling frontispieces.

Also in the Vatican Vergil, by studying offsets of a lost folio we know that Book VII began with a medallion on a recto facing the end of the previous book; this was probably a portrait of Vergil, perhaps following a tradition of decorating rolls with such medallions of authors. Then for the next opening there was at the left a small illustration and four lines of text for the first episode facing five lines and the illustration of the second episode. The irregularity of these systems gives the impression of tentative experiments with the idea of a formal frontispiece but the practice of embedding the illustrations in their proper place in the continuing text, as was obviously convenient in rolls, still rules in the Vatican Vergil and presumably was true of our artist's iconographic model.

The Roman Vergil has more than a simple frontispiece to a text; it has a planned sequence of display pages to mark the transition from one book to another. The first opening in the sequence at the beginning of the *Aeneid* has the last verses of the

Georgics and a colophon at the left and prefatory verses to the *Aeneid* at the right (compare pp. 36-7), the next opening was left blank on both pages to create a visual pause; then came the grand pair of frontispiece illustrations, and after that splendid display a blank verso facing the framed incipit (p. 27). This elaborate sequence of visual effects is the opposite of the close relation of illustration and text in the older tradition, which in earlier codices remained indebted to the limits of the roll format. But if we look forward we realize that the Roman Vergil, by taking full advantage of the possibilities of the codex format, is developing ideas that will flourish in the Middle Ages.

Putting a frame around the text of the first page of the *Aeneid* (p. 27) is a unique invention here, another feature that will be very prominent in the Middle Ages. There was a partial precedent in the lost Calendar of 354, a luxurious book known only from antiquarian copies of a Carolingian copy. This collection of chronological information began with twenty-one pages with enframed symbolic representations of the four chief cities of the empire, the planetary deities (above), and the months of the year. But this frame is derived from wall decoration, and calendars of this kind were frequently engraved on stone. Such a design is intrinsically inappropriate for a page of a book, while the frame in the Roman Vergil has the appropriate scale and gives grand solemnity to the opening of the text, even if it fits rather tightly and is clumsy in detail.

The Roman Vergil has no large decorated initials, but we can find in it hints of the basic impetus to enlarge initials in many first or last lines on a page, and to give the top of an F or the tail of a Q an extra flourish (see pp. 45-6). The first known manuscript with elaborately decorated initials, a feature fundamental for medieval books, is another very pretentious Vergil, called the Augustan Vergil because in 1863 the Berlin librarian G. H. Pertz was so impressed with its grandeur that he thought it dated back to the time of Augustus. There is no precise evidence for its actual date but it probably was made in Rome soon after the Roman Vergil for a patron with a similar desire to show off his admiration for the classics. The parchment is not as fine as in the Roman Vergil, but each page starts with a large coloured initial like the one here on the facing page; only seven folios survive, all from the *Georgics*, none with illustrations, and we may imagine that in his desire for grandeur this patron turned to size and rich decoration rather than to illustration. His book was significantly larger than the Roman Vergil, about 430 x 360 mm instead of the squarer 350 x 335, and filled about 330 folios with the text (assuming no illustrations or accessory texts). The written area (about 250 x 260) is slightly larger than in the Roman Vergil (about 230 x 245) but the margins are extremely generous, including an inner margin of about 38 mm instead of about 25 mm in the Roman Vergil (with slight variations from page to page).

The initials, which vary from 35 to 40 mm in height, always stand up from the base of the first line on the page whereas when initials like these developed later in the sixth century they generally extended further into the left margin and down into the text area. There is an initial in this position whether the first word of a page begins a sentence (as in this illustration) or is in the middle of a phrase. In both these ways one gets the impression here of a first experiment in decorating a page rather than in using an initial to enhance the text, to introduce a new section, as later became the norm.

The initials are all drawn with fine ink lines, using either a straight edge or a compass; when O or Q is the letter (as shows through dimly from the other side of the folio illustrated here) it is based on two circles about 6 mm apart, producing a letter with very marked shading and a vertical axis. The basic geometric form of the initial is then elaborated with small curved terminals, or even very small tendrils, and the body is often filled with a linear pattern of very fine lines, such as the zigzag in this A, a motif very different in character from the calligraphic squiggles used to decorate colophons and prefaces in the Roman Vergil (cf. pp. 36-37). These initials are then partly covered with a coloured wash, but a wash rather carelessly executed, not filling exactly the intended areas. The colours are green (verdigris, which is acidic and tends to eat through the parchment), a little diluted red (probably minium), and a very thin tan (perhaps diluted ink), pigments very different from the thicker and more saturated colours used in the Roman Vergil, but they are the pigments that became customary in Italian manuscripts in the sixth century and spread widely in the Merovingian era.

The initials are all based on Square capital forms in the tradition of the great imperial inscriptions on stone (except for the v-shaped cross stroke of the A), and the script of the text is mostly based on traditional forms, but with exaggerated shading and a geometrical character that comes from using straight lines and segments of circles almost exclusively. The script is written between two lines ruled lightly with a stylus on every flesh side, and the letters observe these limits carefully, with only very slight extensions such as the the top of an L. Letters such as H and N are made almost exactly square while M is restricted in width to be nearly square; similarly B and R are extended to the right so as to occupy an essentially square space. The effect is very different from the more elongated shapes and vertical character of the Roman Vergil script and as a result these letters are about 6 mm high instead of 8 or 9 mm as in the Roman Vergil, and there are twenty lines to a page instead of eighteen.

Most vertical strokes are very broad and the letters O and Q were drawn with nearly vertical shading. But straight diagonal strokes are equally broad, as in the cross stroke of N, made with the pen oriented at 45°; there the vertical strokes are mere hairlines, requiring the pen to be oriented horizontally for a moment. In the S the diagonal stroke is again very broad but this time it is the horizontal strokes that are hair lines. This requires even more changes of angle than in the script of the Roman Vergil. Meanwhile, strangely enough, A has no cross bar and the letters E F L T have the Rustic capital form, with heavier slightly curved horizontal strokes, and are much narrower than they need be. In short this script is a strangely mannered version of the old Square capitals of imperial inscriptions and cannot be considered part of a living tradition, less so than the script of the Roman Vergil. It was an artificial exercise in reviving selected forms, carried out by a very skilful scribe.

The smaller letters in the right margin where the scribe ran out of space and had to restrict himself to finish the verse on one line are generally less formal versions of the main script, but on line 10 there is a curious ligature for OS and line 15 has a ligature for TR; on other pages there are ligatures for NT and VNT, all relatively late symptoms not found in the Roman Vergil.

The ornament used to fill the initials is very modest by comparison with later developments in the sixth century and the few tendril finials are only a timid beginning. Still, here we get the impression of a scribe experimenting with new forms of decoration, going beyond the Roman Vergil, making a start in a direction very important for Medieval art.

A TQ·ALIVSLATVMFVNDAIAMVERBERAIAMNE
ALIAPETENSPELAGOQ·ALIVSTRAHITVMIDALINA
TVMFERRIRIGORATQ·ARGVTAELAMMINASERRAE
NAMPRIMICVNEISSCINDEBANTFISSILELIGNVM
TVMVARIAEVENEREARTESLABOROMNIAVICIT
IMPROBETDVRISSVRGENSINREBNEGESTAS
PRIMACERESFERROMORTALISVERTERETERRAM
INSTITVITCVMIAMGIANDESATQARBVTASACRAE
DEFICERENTSILVAEETVICTVMDODONANEGRET
MOXETFRVMENTISLABORADDITVSVTMALACVLM
ESSETROBIGOSEGNISQ·HORREREINARVISII
CARDVVSINTEREVNTSEGETESSVBITASPERASIL
LAPPAEQ·TRIBOLIQ·INTERQ·NITENTIACVLTV
INFELIXLOLIVMETSTERILESDOMINANTVRAVEN
QVODNISIETADSIDVISTERRAMINSECTABERERASTRIS
ETSONITVTERREBISAVESETRVRISOPACI
FALCEPREMESVMBRASVOTISQ·VOCAVERISIMBRE
HEVMAGNVMALTERIVSFRVSTRASPECTABISACERVVM
CONCVSSAQ·FAMEMINSILVISSOLABEREQVERCV
DICENDVMETQVAESINTDVRISAGRESTIBARMA

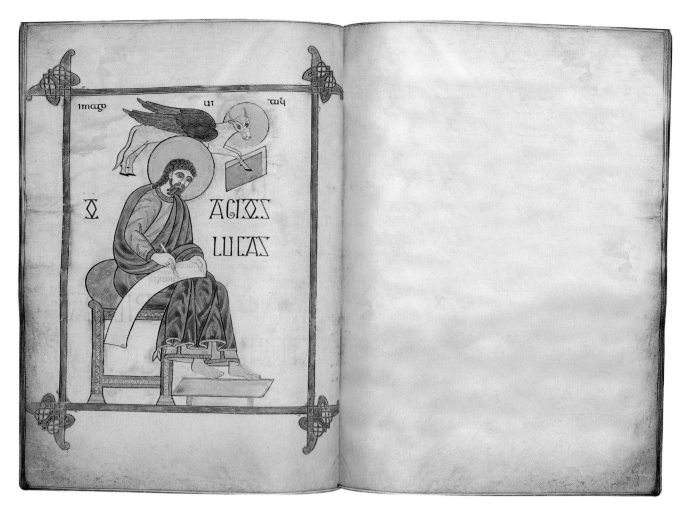

Lindisfarne Gospels open to the portrait of St Luke, c. 700 (BL Cotton Nero D.iv, fols. 137v–138r)

If we skip to the development of display pages in the Book of Durrow and the Lindisfarne Gospels we can see something comparable happening under different circumstances, developing out of non-classical traditions. The Book of Durrow was the first to introduce representational art into the Hiberno-Saxon system: evangelist symbols rendered almost as if they were Anglo-Saxon metalwork. They were considered so foreign that they were isolated in a decorated frame on the left hand page of an opening, facing a blank, followed by the opening with more native roots: the carpet page (probably based on bookbinding designs) at the left and the decorated incipit at the right. A generation later in the Lindisfarne Gospels there are Evangelist portraits based on Italian models but they remain isolated at the left of a separate opening (above) and the subsequent opening for the text becomes ever more elaborate, with an intricate carpet page and a decorated frame expanding on traditions of Anglo-Saxon metalwork added here to enclose the enormous initial and the start of the text (facing page). Of course the Anglo-Saxon artists did not know the Roman Vergil but they did know Italian frontispiece illustrations, as evident from their copy of Cassiodorus's Ezra page in the Codex Amiatinus and their adaptation of it for the Lindisfarne figure of Matthew. Around 700 the idea of a representational image was still so foreign that it must be kept isolated on a separate opening but in the next generation that principle was rejected and in the Gospel Books made at Charlemagne's court the pairing of Evangelist portrait and incipit page produced sumptuous openings with elaborate classical frames (facing page). The legacy of our grandiose experiment in a sequence of display pages for a codex became part of the European tradition.

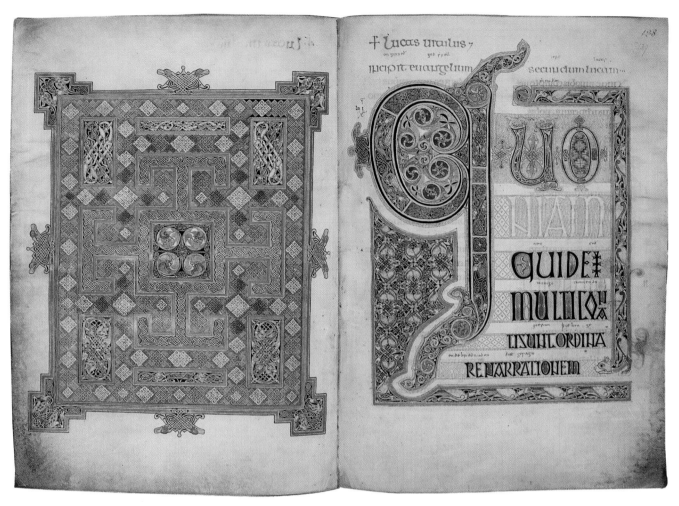

Lindisfarne Gospels open to the incipit of St Luke, c. 700 (BL Cotton Nero D.iv, fols. 138v–139r)

Harley Gospels open to the portrait and incipit of St Luke, c. 800 (BL Harley 2788, fols. 108v–109r)

Our patron was obviously very wealthy at a time when there cannot have been much excess wealth available for art. It was a time of political collapse, with unavoidable economic consequences, but he chose to commission an extraordinarily pretentious copy of the works of the great national poet and he insisted on having his book illustrated. That must have been a rare commission, for only two of the seven known ancient codices of Vergil had illustrations. He found a scriptorium still able to provide superb parchment and calligraphy but he had to accept an inadequate painter. He must have thought it very important to preserve traditional culture and he probably wanted to be admired for doing so. His book was too big to hold and had to be placed on a stand; the illustrations were obviously designed for display whereas the Vatican Vergil was designed to be held for reading, the illustrations to be enjoyed with the text. So we may imagine our patron showing off his new book, placed on its stand, expecting admiration for his patronage of traditional culture.

That makes all the more intriguing the outspokenly pagan content of the Sacrifice in Honour of Anchises and the powerful effect of the Council of the Gods. Our patron must in some way have favoured maintaining pagan traditions and he must have had friends sympathetic to that point of view. Yet repeated imperial edicts had banned pagan sacrifices and an edict of 408 in Rome specifically required the destruction of pagan images. Of course pagan observances did not stop immediately and for a long time we still hear of individual office holders who were pagans; in fact, not until 495 did Pope Gelasius ban the disreputable pagan festival of the Lupercalia, with its sexual overtones, and even than a Christian senator protested at the ban on this popular celebration. We cannot reconstruct our patron's society in detail but we can identify something of his outlook and we may suppose he was not alone.

For the later history of the manuscript, scattered corrections in the text show that the book remained in use in some Italian collection at least into the seventh century, but with the general collapse of classical Roman culture in Italy it must eventually have fallen into neglect. We have no firm evidence, but it is reasonable speculation that it may have been one of the manuscripts collected by Charlemagne when he was in Italy, perhaps at the time of his coronation in 800, and taken to his court in Aachen. Then when his library was dispersed after his death in 814 it seems to have gone to the royal abbey of Saint-Denis, where it certainly was during the Middle Ages. Some monks must have read it there early on, because a unique misspelling in this manuscript (Minoeia for Minoia in *Aeneid* 6.14) is quoted around 865 by Heric of Auxerre in his life of St Germain, but there is no trace of any direct influence of these miniatures on Carolingian art. Its text, on the other hand, was so prized at Saint-Denis that in the twelfth century nearly forty small corrections were carefully written in, a unique case of such scholarly study of an ancient book in that era (see p. 18, last line).

It was still at Saint-Denis when Abbot Jehan Courtoys (1441-43) signed his name in it (see p. 27 at the top), but by 1475 it was listed in the first inventory of the Vatican Library, perhaps changing hands at one of the church councils and acquired by one of the humanists in papal circles. When it appeared in that inventory Cardinal Giuliano della Rovere, the future Pope Julius II, borrowed it for study. Then when the Florentine scholar Poliziano was in Rome in 1484 he studied it and cited its colophons to establish the correct spelling *Vergilius* instead of the medieval *Virgilius*. The Roman scholar Valeriano studied it in detail for his work on the text of Vergil published in 1521 and baptized the manuscript "Codex Romanus" because of the truly Roman quality of its script. Many scholars have made careful studies of its text in subsequent centuries, and it remains a key witness for the scholarly edition of Vergil.

Its illustrations, on the other hand, attracted relatively little attention during the Renaissance. Then in 1633 the antiquarian Cassiano dal Pozzo had eight of the illustrations copied as part of his Paper Museum, intended to be a comprehensive collection of antiquarian copies, and in 1677 Pietro Santi Bartoli published engravings copied from these drawings, not from the actual manuscript (facing page). Such a distorted copy makes it clear that in the seventeenth century even devoted antiquarians found the style of our paintings so degraded that they must be reinterpreted. That attitude continued in effect through the nineteenth century, and even so sensitive a specialist as Franz Wickhoff could suggest that these miniatures were simplified because they were for children. But our eyes trained by the paintings of Matisse, Picasso, and Klee have no trouble reading these images, and with a little tolerance for clumsy workmanship we can see them as important examples of the survival of classical culture at a time when the society supporting that culture was on the verge of collapse.

Pietro Santi Bartoli's engaving of Dido and Aeneas in the Cave, 1677

Roman Vergil (Vat. lat. 3867)

DAVID H. WRIGHT, *Codicological Notes on the Vergilius Romanus*, (Vatican City, 1992) (Studi e Testi 345) gives very detailed technical descriptions of all aspects of the manuscript, including illustrations.

The facsimile *Vergilius Romanus* (Zürich, 1986) has excellent colour reproductions of all twenty illuminated folios at actual size but the rest of the manuscript was reproduced in black and white at 44% actual size from a microfilm that was not quite sharp; the commentary by Carlo Bertelli *et al.* has many errors.

FLORENTINE MÜTHERICH, "Die illustrierten Vergil-Handschriften der Spätantike," *Würzburger Jahrbücher für die Altertumswissenschaft* NF 8 (1982) 205-221, and CHRISTOFF EGGENBERGER, "Die Miniaturen des Vergilius Romanus" *Byzantinische Zeitschrift* 70 (1977) 58-90, are valuable articles.

Vatican Vergil (Vat. lat. 3225)

DAVID H. WRIGHT, *The Vatican Vergil, a Masterpiece of Late Antique Art* (Berkeley, 1993) gives 32 pages in colour and a general discussion.

Vergilius Vaticanus (Codices e Vaticanis Selecti 40; Codices Selecti 71) (Graz, 1980) reproduces the entire book in colour; my commentary volume (1984) gives very detailed descriptions.

Lost Late Antique illustrated Terence

DAVID H. WRIGHT, "The Organization of the Lost Late Antique Illustrated Terence" in *Medieval Manuscripts of the Latin Classics: Production and Use* (edd. Claudine A. Chavannes-Mazel and Margaret M. Smith, Los Altos Hills, 1996) pp. 41-56; my comprehensive monograph will be published soon by the Vatican Library.

WILHELM KOEHLER and FLORENTINE MÜTHERICH, *Die Karolingische Miniaturen*, vol. IV (Berlin, 1971) reproduces all the illustrations of the best copy (Vat. lat. 3868).

Augustan Vergil (Vat. lat. 3256 and Berlin lat. 2° 416)

CARL NORDENFALK, *Vergilius Augusteus*, Graz, 1976 (Codices selecti 66); an excellent facsimile, but Nordenfalk's attempt to date the manuscript in the fourth century is not widely accepted.

Papyrus style

DAVID H. WRIGHT, "The Inheritance of the Papyrus Style of Illustration in Early Latin Literary Codices," *Dumbarton Oaks Papers* 50 (1996) 199-208.

KURT WEITZMANN, *Illustrations in Roll and Codex* (Princeton, 1947; 2nd ed. 1970) and *Ancient Book Illumination* (Cambridge, Mass., 1959) are the fundamental studies, treating mostly Greek material.

COLIN H. ROBERTS and T. C. Skeat, *The Birth of the Codex* (London, 1983), gives a systematic survey of the sources and of the surviving material (mostly Greek papyri found in Egypt); no discussion of illustrations.

Palaeography

BERNHARD BISCHOFF, *Latin Palaeography, Antiquity and the Middle Ages* (Cambridge, 1990), the most authoritative general guide to codicology and to Latin scripts.

MICHELLE P. BROWN, *A Guide to Western Historical Scripts from Antiquity to 1600*, (London & Toronto, 1990, rev. ed. 1994), a very helpful introduction.

MICHELLE P. BROWN and PATRICIA LOVETT, *The Historical Source Book for Scribes,* (London & Toronto, 1999), especially pp. 21-37.

ELIAS AVERY LOWE, *Codices Latini Antiquiores* (Oxford, 12 vols. 1934-69), detailed descriptions and samples of script of all known Latin manuscripts up to 800.

JEAN MALLON, ROBERT MARICHAL, CHARLES PICARD, *L'Ecriture latine de la capitale romaine à la minuscule*, (Paris, 1939), excellent plates of selected extracts, with transcriptions.

CARL NORDENFALK, *Die spätantiken Zierbuchstaben*, (Stockholm, 1970), a very valuable corpus of material.

Vedere i Classici, l'illustrazione libraria dei testi dall'età romana al tardo medio evo, (Rome, 1996); a beautifully illustrated exhibition catalogue.

History of art

ERNST KITZINGER, *Byzantine Art in the Making* (London and Cambridge, Mass., 1977), a balanced survey from the third century through the seventh but very little on manuscripts.

BEAT BRENK, *Die frühchristliche Mosaïken in S. Maria Maggiore zu Rom* (Wiesbaden, 1975), the most authoritative analysis; to be used with the illustrations in Heinrich Karpp, *Die frühchristliche und mittelalterlichen Mosaïken in S. Maggiore zu Rom* (Baden-Baden, 1966).

RICHARD DELBRÜCK, *Die Consulardiptychen und verwandte Denkmäler* (Berlin, 1929), the authoritative corpus publication; Wolfgang F. Volbach, *Elfenbein Arbeiten der Spätantike und des frühen Mittelalters* (Mainz, 2nd ed. 1952; 3rd ed. 1976) can be used when Delbrück is not available.

FRIEDRICH W. DEICHMANN, *Frühchristiliche Bauten und Mosaïken von Ravenna* (Baden-Baden, 1958; reprint Wiesbaden, n.d.) for illustrations and *Ravenna, Haupstadt des spätantiken Abendlandes*, vol. I (Wiesbaden, 1969) for full discussion.

JOSEPH WILPERT, *Römische Mosaiken und Malereien der kirchlichen Bauten vom IV. Bis XIII. Jahrhundert*, (Freiburg, 1916); with excellent colour plates specially made to distinguish between original parts and repairs or restorations.

JONATHAN J.G. ALEXANDER, *Insular Manuscripts, 6th to the 9th century*, (London, 1978).

Historical background

ROGER COLLINS, *Early Medieval Europe 300-1000*, (London, 1991); a systematic survey.

AVERIL CAMERON, *The Mediterranean World in Late Antiquity AD 395-600*, (London, 1993); a stimulating introduction to the period.

LEIGHTON D. REYNOLDS and NIGEL G. WILSON, *Scribes and Scholars, a Guide to the Transmission of Greek and Latin Literature*, (Oxford, 3rd ed. 1991).

DAVID H. WRIGHT, "The Persistence of Pagan Art patronage in Fifth-Century Rome", Aetos, *Studies in Honour of Cyril Mango*, (Stuttgart, 1998), pp. 354-369.

© 2001 David H. Wright

First published 2001 by
The British Library
96 Euston Road
London NWI 2DB

Published in North and South America by
University of Toronto Press Incorporated, Toronto and Buffalo

Canadian Cataloguing in Publication Data

Wright, David H. (David Herndon)
The Roman Vergil and the origins of the medieval book design

Copublished by the British Library.
ISBN 0-8020-4819-6

1. Vergilius - Romanus. 2. Virgil - Manuscripts. 3. Illumination of books and
manuscripts, Roman. 4. Manuscripts, Latin - Vatican City. 5. Virgil -
Illustrations.
I. British Library. II. Title

PA6825.W747 2001   745.6'7'09376   C99-932828-X

Designed and typeset by Centro Tibaldi, Milan
Printed in Italy

MY DAD ALWAYS SAID, WHEN THE TOWNSPEOPLE FORGET ABOUT THE DEADLY FOG, IT MEANS THE DAM KEEPER HAS DONE HIS JOB.

SPLASH!

HE PASSED MANY THINGS ON TO ME.

THIS PLANT HE GAVE ME IS ONE OF MY EARLIEST MEMORIES.

IT WAS MY FIRST LESSON.

HE TAUGHT ME CARING IS RESPONSIBILITY.

HE BELIEVED THE WORLD
COULD STILL BE SAVED.

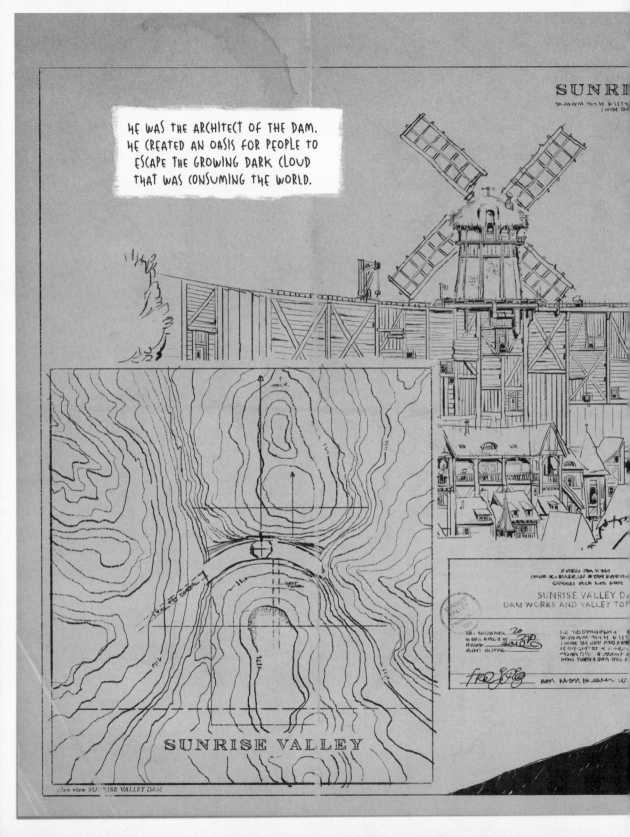

HE WAS THE ARCHITECT OF THE DAM. HE CREATED AN OASIS FOR PEOPLE TO ESCAPE THE GROWING DARK CLOUD THAT WAS CONSUMING THE WORLD.

SUNRISE VALLEY

SUNRISE VALLEY DAM
DAM WORKS AND VALLEY TOP

plan view SUNRISE VALLEY DAM

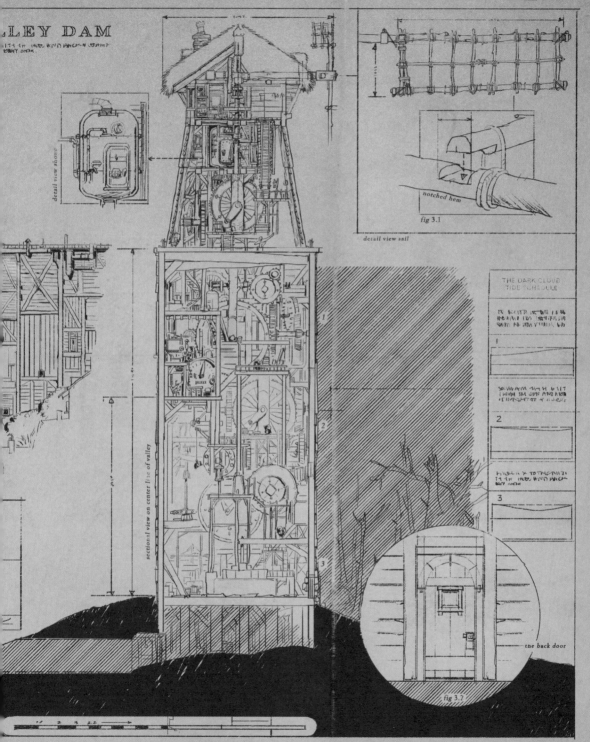

LLEY DAM

detail view stone

detail view sail

notched hem

fig 3.1

sectional view on center line of valley

THE DARK CLOUD
TIDE SCHEDULE

1

2

3

the back door

fig 3.2

HE SHOWED ME ALL I NEEDED TO KNOW TO RUN THE DAM.

HOW TO READ AND MAINTAIN IT.

WHERE TO GO TO FIX A PIPE...

...OR ADJUST PRESSURE.

HE ALSO WARNED ME WHERE NOT TO GO.

MY DAD TAUGHT ME TO WIND THE DAM.

I WAS A SMALL KID, SO IT TOOK
EVERYTHING I HAD, BUT I LEARNED.

ONCE I WAS READY, HE GAVE ME A GREAT RESPONSIBILITY: TO KEEP THE DAM.

IT WAS MY PROUDEST MOMENT.

RING! RING!

The giant fan atop the dam stops every twelve hours.

The deadly fog rolls in like an ocean tide.

I HAVE TO WIND UP THE DAM TO BLOW THE FOG BACK OUT.

FWOOSH

FWOOSH

KUN

UN

THE JOB OF A DAM KEEPER IS TO KEEP THE DARKNESS AWAY.

I AM THE DAM KEEPER.

the
DAM KEEPER
BOOK ONE

ROBERT KONDO
DAISUKE "DICE" TSUTSUMI

:01
First Second
NEW YORK

I AM NOT CRAZY.

I AM NOT LIKE HIM.

I HAVE KEPT MY PROMISE.

I HAVE UPHELD MY RESPONSIBILITIES.

THE PEOPLE ARE SAFE.

I ACCEPT MY PLACE AS THE WALL STANDING BETWEEN THE FOG AND THE TOWN.

A TOWN WHERE I OTHERWISE DON'T BELONG.

EVEN IF THEY HAVE FORGOTTEN.

EVERYONE ACTS WEIRD, TRYING SO HARD TO FIT IN.

I IMAGINE IT IS ONLY GOING TO GET WORSE AS WE GROW OLDER.

BUT I'VE SETTLED INTO MY PLACE.

I HAVE SOMEONE I CAN ALWAYS COUNT ON.

YUCK!

She's been there for me since she came to our town when we were nine years old.

IN MY DARKEST DAYS, SHE HELPED ME TO SEE THE LIGHT.

SHE'S MY BEST FRIEND.

HEY, FOXY!

BUT I'M NOT HER ONLY BEST FRIEND.

TWO FOR FLINCHING!

SOME THINGS NEVER CHANGE, EH, PIG?

YOU GOTTA BE CRAZY LIKE YOUR POPS TO GO UP AGAINST ME.

DUDE, IF WE'RE GONNA HANG THIS SUMMER, YOU NEED TO CHILL.

OH, YEAH, RIGHT. SORRY, DIRT...

ALRIGHTY, FOXY, I'LL TELL YOU MORE ABOUT MARY TOMORROW OVER SOME S'MORES.

FSSSH...

FSSSH...

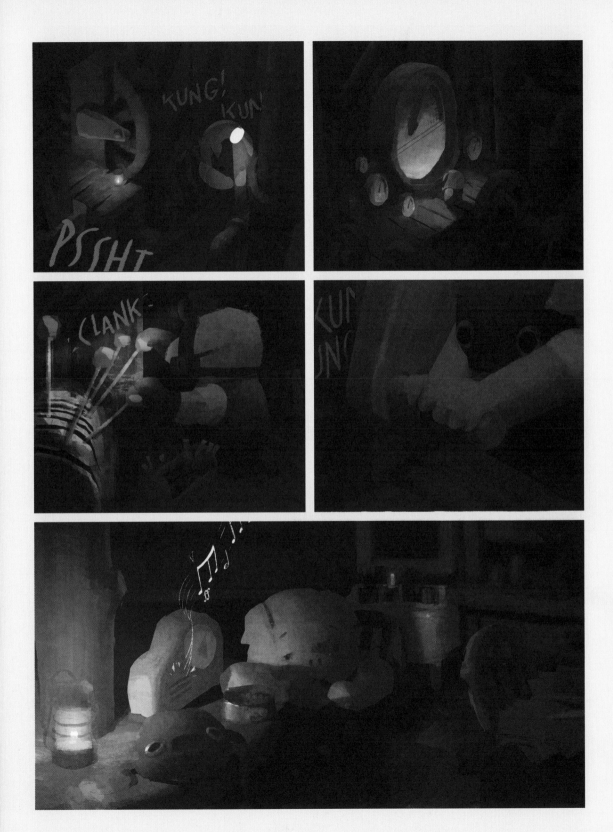

THE SUMMER MEANS TIME TO MYSELF.

I CAN FOCUS ON THE DAM, MAINTAINING THE GEARS AND CHECKING THE METERS. THERES NO PRETENDING TO FIT IN. JUST TIME SPENT HERE. WHERE I BELONG.

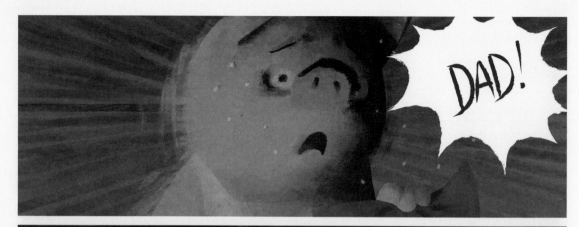

I'VE NEVER SEEN THE LAND WITHOUT THE FOG.

WHEN THE WAVE RETURNS, IT COMES BACK MORE POWERFUL EACH TIME.

CRASH!

WHAT'S GOING ON WITH THE FOG?

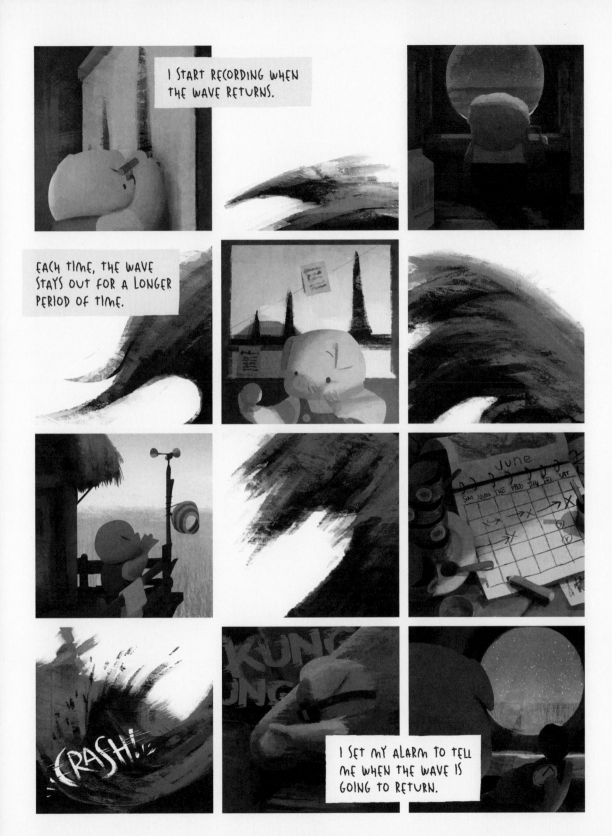

I START RECORDING WHEN THE WAVE RETURNS.

EACH TIME, THE WAVE STAYS OUT FOR A LONGER PERIOD OF TIME.

CRASH!

I SET MY ALARM TO TELL ME WHEN THE WAVE IS GOING TO RETURN.

I LOOK THROUGH MY DAD'S OLD JOURNALS. HE MAY HAVE BEEN CRAZY, BUT NOBODY KNEW THE FOG LIKE HE DID.

THERE MIGHT BE ANSWERS HERE.

BUT I DON'T FIND ANYTHING.

...zz...ZZZ...zz...

KNOCK KNOCK KNOCK

THERE'S A LOT OF STRANGE THINGS GOING ON WITH THE FOG.

YEAH? LIKE WHAT?

...

IT'S SO COOL IN HERE, FOXY. WHAT'S ALL THIS STUFF?

WHAT?

WHY IS HE HERE?

I THOUGHT YOU TWO COULD FINALLY SPEND SOME TIME GETTING TO KNOW EACH OTHER. PLUS HIPPO'S NEVER SEEN THE FOG UP CLOSE...

YOU KNOW THE RULES...

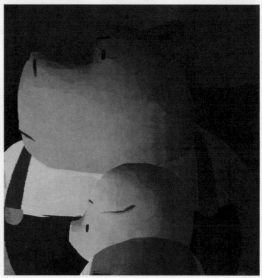

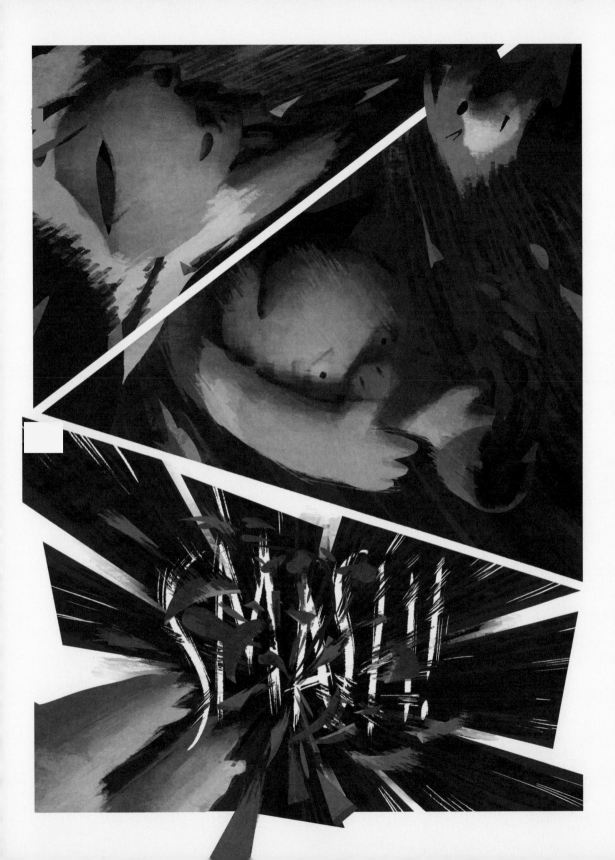

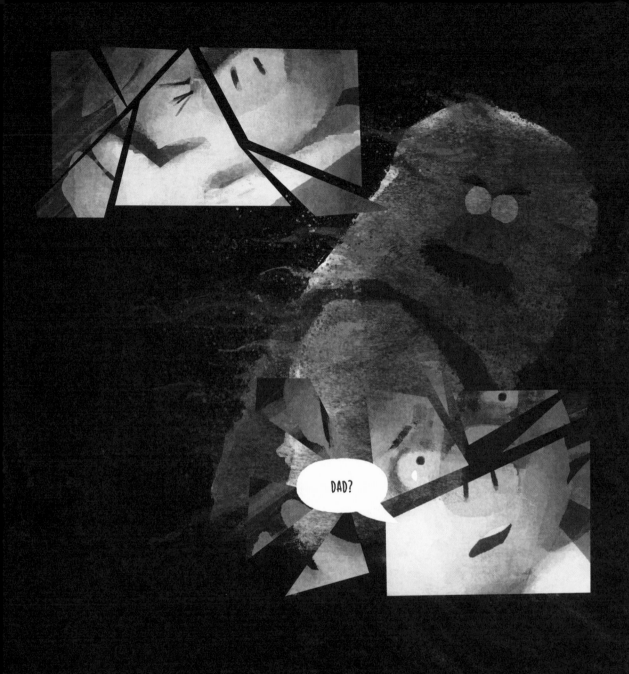

MAYBE SHE'S HURT. SHE MIGHT HAVE BEEN TOSSED OUTSIDE. WE NEED TO GO CHECK.

GO OUTSIDE?! ARE YOU NUTS?

CHECK UNDER THE DEBRIS IN HERE. AND I WILL GO OUTSIDE BY MYSELF.

THROUGH THAT DOOR IS SUICIDE!

I NEED TO SEE THE DAMAGE FROM THE OUTSIDE. THEN WE CAN DECIDE WHAT TO DO!

YOU CRAZY SWINE!

YOU BIG BULLY! CREAK

83

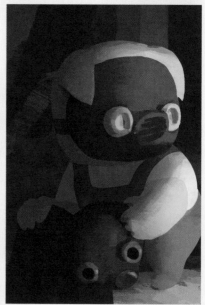

GRABBED THIS FOR YOU.

THANKS, PIG. BUT I DON'T NEED IT. TAKE A LOOK OUTSIDE.

BUT AREN'T WE ON THE OTHER SIDE OF THE DAM...IN THE FOG?

C'MON. WE NEED TO HEAD TOWARD THE EARLY MORNING SUN. IT'LL LEAD US BACK TO SUNRISE VALLEY. FOLLOW ME.

JUST REMEMBER THAT NO ONE'S EVER COME OUT HERE AND SURVIVED. LET'S TRY TO STAY ALIVE AND GET HOME BEFORE THE FOG TAKES US.

TAKE IT EASY, PAL. THE BIG GUY SCARES EASY.

WE NEED TO HELP EACH OTHER GET THROUGH THIS.

HEY! EARTH TO HIPPO! WHERE'D YOU GO, BIG GUY? YOU STILL THINKING ABOUT THAT GIRL?

HA, YEAH, SHE MUST BE SO WORRIED ABOUT ME RIGHT NOW, THAT POOR GIRL!

YOU WISH! HAHAHA!!!

94

SHUFFLE...SHUFFle

SHUFFLE...SHUFFle

95

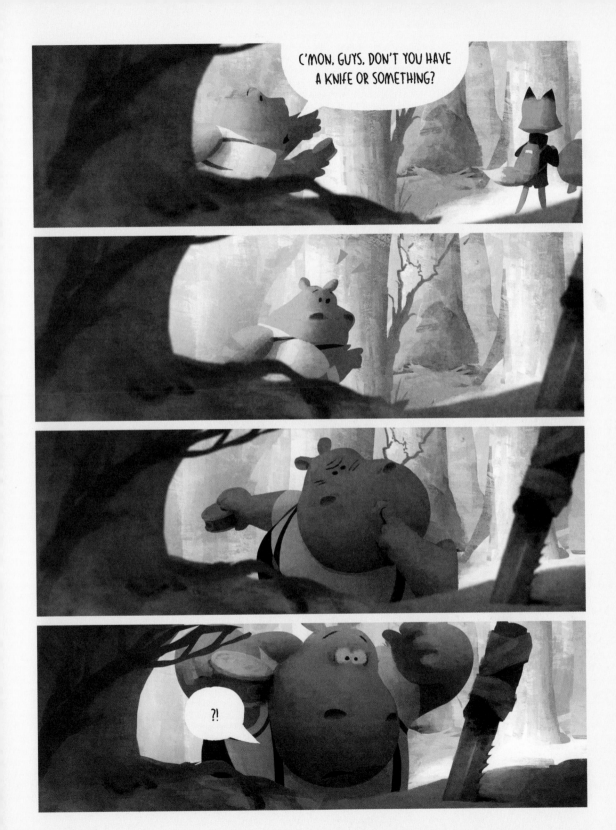

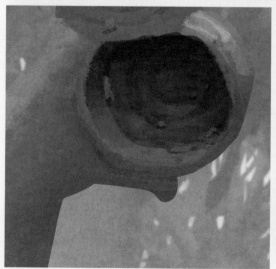

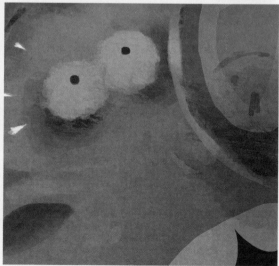

GULP...

IS IT DEAD?

YEAH. LOOKS LIKE HE DIDN'T MAKE IT IN THE FOG.

I FEEL THAT TUNA COMIN' BACK UP. THAT IS THE UGLIEST FROG I HAVE EVER SEEN.

VAN IS NO HARM.

NEPHEWS PASS KNIFE UP HERE.

VAN'S BEEN CHASED BY THE FOG...

...AND IT'S COMING BACK...

YOU HAVE TO CUT VAN DOWN...

113

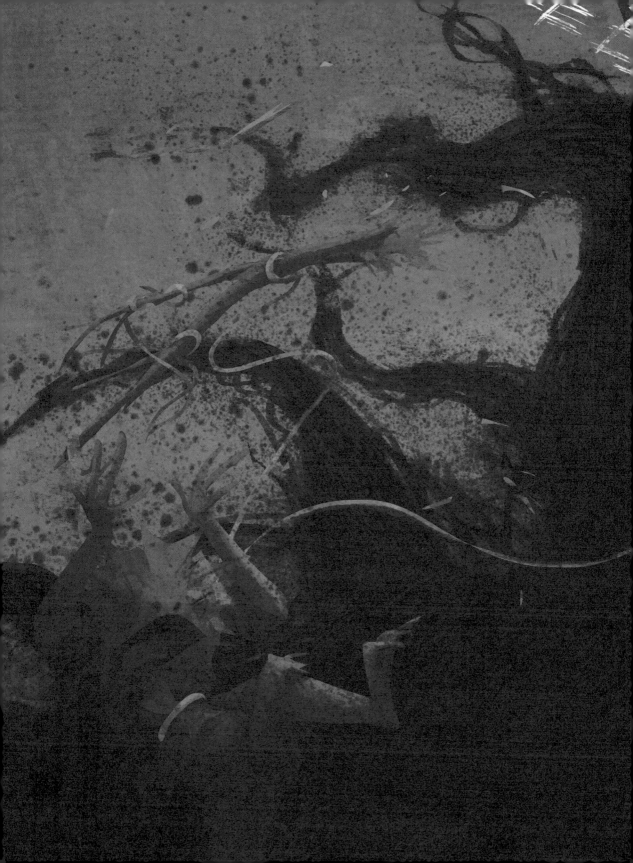

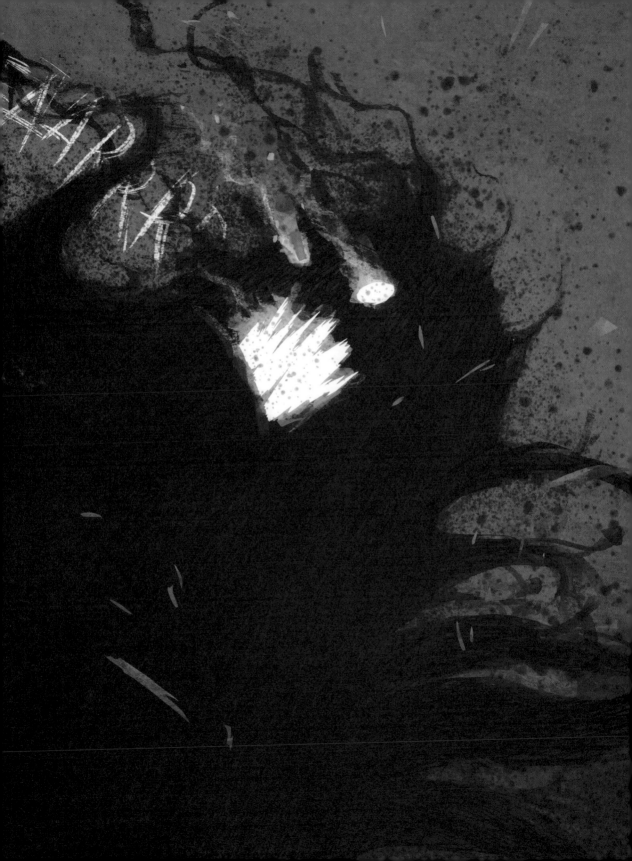

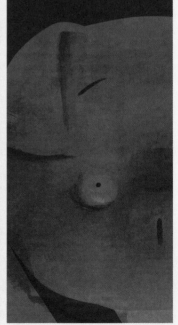

VAN KNOWS THE WAY!

VAN CAN TAKE YOU BACK, JUST NEED VAN'S TRUCK.

NEED TO FIND A SAFE PLACE TO REST FOR THE NIGHT.

YEAH!

POP

FOLLOW VAN! VAN SPOTTED THE PERFECT PLACE WHEN HE WAS HANGING OUT!

IS IT THAT BIG HOLLOW TREE DOWN THERE?

SURE.

DUDES. IT'S DANK IN HERE.

NOT TO HIPPO'S LIKING?

NO, IT'S NOT. WE ARE NOT YOUR FAMILY. OUR FAMILIES ARE WAITING FOR US BACK HOME.

AND I DON'T TRUST YOU.

HIPPO REMINDS ME OF MY SIXTH SON, VAN THE SEVENTH. HARD SHELL OUTSIDE, SOFT AND CUDDLY INSIDE...VAN LIKES NEPHEW HIPPO.

STILL CAN'T BELIEVE WE FOUND HIM OUT HERE. THAT MEANS HE'S LIVED IN THIS FOG.

YEAH, I THOUGHT NOTHING COULD SURVIVE OUT HERE.

I KNOW YOU DON'T REALLY TALK ABOUT THIS MUCH. DO YOU THINK YOUR FATHER COULD'VE SURVIVED?

...NO, THERE'S NO WAY.

...BESIDES, EVEN IF HE DID, WHAT DIFFERENCE WOULD IT MAKE?

I'M SCARED, PIG. WHAT IF WE NEVER SEE OUR FAMILIES AGAIN?

DON'T WORRY, FOX. WE WILL GET HOME. WE HAVE NINE DAYS UNTIL THE NEXT WAVE HITS.

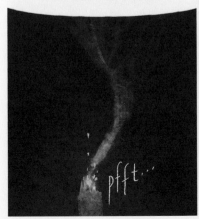

GET SOME REST. TOMORROW MR. VAN WILL TAKE US HOME. WE SHOULD TRY TO GET SOME SLEEP...

pfft...

YEAH, GOOD NIGHT, BUD.

GOOD NIGHT, FOX.

fwoosh...

zzᶻzzz...

DAD?

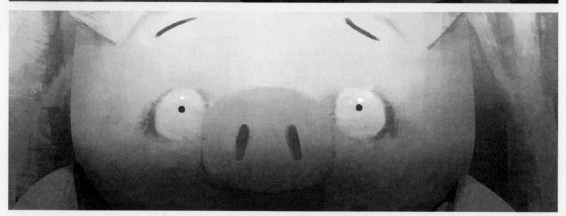

KUNG KUNG KUNG KUNG KUNG KUNG KUNG KUNG KUNG

DUDES, IT'S STILL TOO EARLY AND YOU KNOW I'M NOT A MORNING GUY.

...OH MY...

WHOA...

JUST LIKE OUR TOWN'S, EXCEPT THIS ONE'S HUMONGOUS.

THE WINDMILLS ARE MOVING. DO YOU THINK SOMEONE IS LIVING IN THERE?

KUNG...KUNG...K

MY JOB IS TO KEEP
THE DARKNESS AWAY.

I AM THE DAM KEEPER.

The adventure continues in . . .

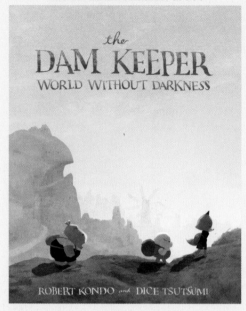

the
DAM KEEPER
WORLD WITHOUT DARKNESS

ROBERT KONDO and DICE TSUTSUMI

Special thanks to John Henry Hinkel, Bradley Furnish, Mark Siegel, Robyn Chapman, Andrew Arnold, Gina Gagliano, the entire team at First Second, and Macmillan Publishers.

:01
First Second

Copyright © 2017 by Tonko House Inc.

Published by First Second
First Second is an imprint of Roaring Brook Press, a
division of Holtzbrinck Publishing Holdings Limited Partnership
175 Fifth Avenue, New York, New York 10010
All rights reserved

Library of Congress Control Number: 2016961560

ISBN 978-1-62672-426-6

Our books may be purchased in bulk for promotional, educational, or business use.
Please contact your local bookseller or the Macmillan Corporate and Premium Sales Department
at (800) 221-7945 ext. 5442 or by e-mail at MacmillanSpecialMarkets@macmillan.com.

FIRST
EDITION

First edition 2017
Book design by John Green and Andrew Arnold

Printed in China by RR Donnelley Asia Printing Solutions Ltd., Dongguan City, Guangdong Province

Penciled with Shiyoon Kim's Wet Ink brush and painted with
Tonko House's custom paintbrush in Adobe Photoshop.

1 3 5 7 9 10 8 6 4 2

BY ART
WE LIVE